Marylanders
of the
Century

Other books from *The Sun*:

The Great Game of Maryland Politics by Barry Rascovar

Are We There Yet? Recollections of Life's Many Journeys
by Elise T. Chisolm

The Ultimate Guide to Baltimore Schools

Miss Prudence Pennypack's Perfectly Proper
by Karen E. Rupprecht

A Century In The Sun: Photographs of Maryland

A Century In The Sun: Front Pages of the 20th Century

A Century In The Sun: Postcards of Maryland's Past

*Dining in Baltimore: Food And Drink In
And Around Charm City*

*Hometown Boy: The Hoodle Patrol and Other Curiosities
of Baltimore*, by Rafael Alvarez

*The Wild Side of Maryland, An Outdoor Guide,
2nd Edition*

*Gaining A Yard: The Building of Baltimore's
Football Stadium* by Jon Morgan and Doug Kapustin

Raising Kids & Tomatoes by Rob Kasper

Motherhood Is A Contact Sport by Susan Reimer

Cal Touches Home

This *Sun* book was published by SunSource, the information service of *The Sun*. To order
any of the above titles, or for information on research, reprints and information from the
paper's archives, please call 410.332.6800.

Marylanders
of the
Century

edited by Barry Rascovar

THE BALTIMORE SUN

Published by
The Baltimore Sun
A Times-Mirror company
501 N. Calvert Street
Baltimore, MD 21278

Edited by Barry Rascovar
Layout and design by Jennifer Halbert

ISBN – 1-893116-11-5
Library of Congress publication data applied for.

Marylanders of the Century: a publication of the Baltimore Sun Company - 1999 - Baltimore, MD: Baltimore Sun Co.: 1999

400282 | 61060

Contents

Introduction

ONE HUNDRED YEARS. 1900 to 2000. Ten decades. Two or three generations in a family's life span.

Massive social and political transformations have taken place over the past 1,200 months. The United States entered 1900 as a second-rate power. It ends the century as *the* world power, preeminent in technology, in military might and in the strength of its economy and its democracy.

Maryland, too, has been transformed. Half of all Marylanders lived in Baltimore as the century began. Indeed, Baltimore *was* Maryland in many respects. But the advent of the automobile changed all that, creating one of the most highly suburbanized states in America.

Few of us remember what it was like in the early part of this century. Our memories are only a generation old. That makes capturing the essence of the past 100 years even more elusive.

Still, the editorial board of *The Sun* set out to identify some of the people who contributed the most to Baltimore and Maryland — if not the nation and world — over this vast time period. It proved a daunting task. So many men and women qualified as Marylanders of the Century. So many lasting accomplishments merited recognition. But in the end, the list was narrowed to just 21 names.

It's not an all-inclusive list, or one that emerged after consulting with hundreds of learned experts from across the state. No, this is a more personal compilation by editorial board members after lengthy discussions over who should make the final cut.

Part One of this book contains the 21 editorials, plus an introductory piece, that ran on *The Sun's* editorial pages under the heading, "Marylanders of the Century."

It's a good starting point for sizing up the last 100 years in our state's history.

To add different perspectives, 16 other *Sun* writers, former and present, were asked to contribute their thoughts. The essays they submitted are contained in Part Two. Three other articles that ran on *The Sun's* Opinion-Commentary page also have been included to round out the section.

If some readers feel this book focuses too heavily on individuals from Baltimore, that's because Maryland's 20th century has been Baltimore-centric. Even in its current decline, Baltimore remains, in many respects, this state's focal point. The advent of suburban living is a relatively recent phenomenon.

There's another reason for Baltimoreans dominating these lists: The writers of these essays have followed the exploits of local personalities for some or all of the past half-century as reporters and columnists for *The Sun*. Those profiled made deep and lasting impressions.

With a few exceptions, the men and women recognized in this book achieved their greatest successes in the post-World War II period. For most of us, the time before then is Ancient History. Our memories are short. We leave it to scholars to establish the full pantheon of Marylanders who warrant inclusion on a 100-year list.

It's not surprising that a number of contributors to this book view the defining issue in Maryland's 20th century as the civil-rights struggle of African Americans. The Civil War of the 19th century, bloody as it was, did not give blacks equal protection and opportunities. That didn't start to happen in earnest until after World War II. The issue has dogged Americans — and Marylanders — throughout this century, just as it did the last.

This book celebrates human accomplishment. It celebrates the good deeds of meritorious Marylanders in many aspects of life. They made a monumental difference through their work. They had an impact that will last for decades and generations to come. We can, and must, build on what they have accomplished.

Those who craft editorials labor in obscurity. That goes with the job. But this book is an occasion for each editorial writer to share a little glory, however briefly. Marylanders of the Century was a team effort. And, as usual, *The Sun's* editorial-page writers produced memorable work.

Daniel Berger wrote the introductory editorial, plus essays on Henry Walters and Walter Sondheim. Lane Harvey Brown wrote editorials on Claire McCardell and David Lewis. Michael K. Burns produced the Helen Taussig editorial. Marilyn McCraven is the writer of the Lillie Carroll Jackson editorial.

Antero Pietila penned the essay on Theodore R. McKeldin. Barry Rascovar authored the Albert Ritchie and William Preston Lane editorials. Andrew Ratner wrote on Harry Kelley, Cal Ripken and Babe Ruth. C. Fraser Smith submitted essays on H. L. Mencken, E. Brooke Lee and William Donald Schaefer. Brian Sullam produced editorials on Abel Wolman, Jacob Blaustein and Charles P. McCormick. Editorial Page Editor Jacqueline Thomas wrote the Eubie Blake editorial. Norris P. West contributed editorials on James Rouse and Thurgood Marshall. Also lending assistance were Stephen Henderson, Franz Schneiderman, Laurie Ann Tagliarini and the always helpful Marc Block.

Four highly skilled artists participated in the creation of this editorial series. Their drawings, included in this book, truly bring these 21 Marylanders of the Century alive. Editorial cartoonist Kevin Kallaugher sketched renderings of Eubie Blake, Lillie Carroll Jackson, David Lewis, Babe Ruth, Walter Sondheim, Helen Taussig and Henry Walters. *The Sun's* other fine editorial cartoonist, Mike Lane, contributed drawings of Claire McCardell, H. L. Mencken, Cal Ripken, James Rouse and William Donald Schaefer. Palden Hamilton, a talented summer intern in the editorial department, drew sketches of William Preston Lane, E. Brooke Lee and Charles P. McCormick. Charles R. "Hap" Hazard, a former artist for *The Sun*, contributed drawings of Jacob Blaustein, Harry Kelley, Thurgood Marshall, Theodore McKeldin, Albert Ritchie and Abel Wolman.

Writers of essays in Part Two also deserve a note of gratitude: Rafael Alvarez, John Bainbridge, Mike Bowler, Jonathan Bor, James Bready, John Dorsey, Sara Engram, Tom Horton, Joan Jacobson, Gregory Kane, Peter Kumpa, Glenn McNatt, Michael Olesker, Hal Piper, Fred Rasmussen, Dan Rodricks, Bill Salganik and Joe Sterne. Over the years they have been my journalistic colleagues at *The Sun* — and sometimes competitors. They are true authorities on the Baltimore and Maryland scene.

Finally, Debbie Golumbek, Laura Gamble and Jennifer Halbert of SunSource deserve thanks for their efforts to make this book a reality. It couldn't have happened without them.

We at *The Sun* hope you find the pages that follow a "good read." It's been a momentous 100 years. Here are the people we think best qualify as Marylanders of the Century.

Barry Rascovar

Baltimore, Maryland
November, 1999

The cream of the crop, in our own estimation

AS THE 20th century draws to its conclusion, the time arrives to honor those whose efforts made life better not just for those around them but for multitudes unknown to them.

How contemporary it would be to claim that this is an objective, computer-compiled list of measurable contributions with quantifiable benefits. Sorry. Can't be done. This is a subjective list, argued and re-argued by The Sun's editorial board. It was compiled by a process not unlike election endorsements or choice of Marylander of the Year — equally scientific, no more and no less. What follows, in short, is this editorial board's opinion.

Arriving at it has been fun and a learning experience. Anyone can play.

To qualify, honorees must be Marylanders. That prompts the question: Maryland-bred or late-comers, people who began here or who ended here? To which the answer can only be, "Yes."

The contributions of these men and women must be positive. There is a place for people who were famous merely for being famous, whose misbehavior defined an era or whose ouevre symbolized the Age of Anxiety. But not here. These Marylanders of the Century have done good. Some did it early in the century; a few are still at it.

Each is unique in contribution, not a representative of a class. Each is substantial in contribution. Some are household names, some more obscure. Some are relatively provincial, their contribution felt most strongly in a region of the state. Others gave to the nation and the world. Many of our selections blur that distinction.

All have made contributions that last and will be remembered, even a century from now.

Marylanders
of the
Century

as selected by The Sun's editorial board

H. L. Mencken, bard of Baltimore

Journalist: No Maryland writer in this century
has matched his power and influence

H. L. MENCKEN WAS a cultural and intellectual phenomenon who transcended his roots to become a fearsome critic of national affairs — yet he remained a fiercely devoted Baltimorean.

Newspaper columnist, magazine editor, prolific author, nurturer of writing talent and celebrity, he always chose Union Square over Broadway.

"Coming back to Baltimore [from New York] is like coming out of a football crowd into quiet communion with a fair one," he wrote.

Along with blue crabs, marble steps and Johns Hopkins Hospital, Mencken put Baltimore on the map in the early decades of the century. If the city had produced a Mencken, it could hardly be as boring as its tedious blocks of row houses sometimes suggested.

A prodigy who had no formal education after Polytechnic High School, Henry Louis Mencken turned into the master essayist of his time — as well as a mentor, admirer or friend to F. Scott Fitzgerald, Sinclair Lewis, James T. Farrell, Theodore Dreiser and other American writers.

Walter Lippmann called him "the most powerful influence on a whole generation of educated Americans."

"The third most fascinating man in the world," according to one poll in the 1920s. Most fascinating, according to another. Movie stars loved his attention as much as politicians loathed it.

As driven as he was masterful, Mencken took his craft to a pinnacle of focused and hilarious acerbity. Columnists since have seldom had his bite or wit or daring.

Mencken, a resident of the 1500 block of Hollins Street for most of his 75 years, endured a brief apprenticeship at his father's cigar factory before presenting himself at the old *Baltimore Morning Herald* — night after night until he landed a job.

About seven years later, at the age of 25, he became the *Herald's* editor in chief. He left the *Herald* to work briefly for the *News American* and then for *The Sun* and *Evening Sun*, where he remained for 40 years.

He was an extraordinary writer of satire and polemic. The owners of *The Sun* saw him as welcome antidote to the "flatulence" of newspaper writing.

As a critic, his subjects were literature, society and ideas. He wrote books on the German philosopher Nietzsche; on democracy; on the American language; the playwright George Bernard Shaw, whose outsider viewpoints he adopted; and his own life and times.

He became editor of two literary journals that ruled the intellectual roost in the 1920s and 1930s: *Smart Set* and *American Mercury*.

He suspected politicians, scorned reformers and found little to recommend the South. His commentary from the Scopes monkey trial is still cited as a prime example of searing social criticism.

Forty-three years after his death, Mencken is still quoted prominently — even during the impeachment trial of President Clinton.

He was skewered for use of derogatory terms for Jews and African-Americans, but his writing suggests he used them in an arch way — in jest or as commentary on the masses who used them derisively.

Many of his friends were Jewish. Black writers have found in Mencken's iconoclasm a model for their own critiques of American society.

Decades before discrimination and bigotry were widely decried, Mencken was taking Maryland and Baltimore to task for appalling attitudes toward and treatment of blacks.

Blemishes and all, he was a leading figure of 20th-century Maryland. His writing career, his enormous influence on American journalism and literature and his loyalty to Baltimore are unparalleled.

Perhaps, as he said, many Baltimoreans "regard Douglas Fairbanks a greater man than Beethoven." But what was that against an atmosphere conducive to long friendships and comfortable, sustaining habits — lunch at Marconi's, dinner at Schellhase's and meetings in the old Rennert Hotel?

His office was in New York, he pointed out repeatedly, but his "being" was in Baltimore.

Thurgood Marshall, justice for all

Supreme Court: Civil rights attorney and judge took lead in cases that shattered segregation

NO ONE HAS done more to energize the civil rights movement and improve race relations in the United States than Thurgood Marshall. The Baltimore native was a juggernaut smashing through the obstacles of racial injustice.

Long before Martin Luther King Jr. and others took to the streets to appeal to the American conscience, Marshall won the crucial battles that built, block by block, the legal pillars of monumental change. He will be remembered as the first African-American Supreme Court justice, but his most important contributions to society came decades before.

As a lawyer for the National Association for the Advancement of Colored People, Marshall secured voting rights for African-Americans, railed against racially motivated criminal charges, stood behind black soldiers facing unfair charges in the military and argued the most significant Supreme Court case of the century — Brown vs. Board of Education.

Only desegregation, he fervently believed, could cure the nation's racial virus.

For well more than half of this century, laws in the South prohibited African-Americans from using the same public accommodations as whites — in spite of the Constitution's guarantee of equal protection. Black people had to use separate schools, public restrooms and water fountains. Black travelers on public conveyances had to move to segregated sections when they crossed the Mason-Dixon Line. Jim Crow's ubiquitous face appeared in restaurants, hotels, movie theaters — even churches.

Marshall graduated from a segregated public school in West Baltimore. He wanted to attend the University of Maryland Law School but didn't bother to apply because he knew he would be rejected because of his race.

He set out to change this soon after graduating from Howard University Law School, where he studied under the renowned Charles Houston.

With the legislative and executive branches of government indifferent to racism, he turned to the courts to prove that separate facilities for whites and blacks were inherently unequal under the law.

His first victory occurred in Baltimore.

He took UM's law school to court and won admission for Donald Murray, a black man, in 1935. It was a major triumph, but only the start for Marshall.

He went on to win a remarkable string of civil rights cases. His crusade sometimes meant risking personal safety — a lynch mob once chased him in Tennessee.

Marshall was a tall, suave figure who relied on research and elegant moral persuasion.

He won over Supreme Court justices, who rarely heard presentations from black lawyers, and triumphed in 29 of his 32 high court cases as an NAACP lawyer.

The biggest, the Brown case, not only ended legal segregation of schools but gave the burgeoning civil rights movement the ammunition to fight for equality in the workplace, housing, politics and economic affairs.

Maryland and the United States are better off because Thurgood Marshall led the NAACP's groundbreaking efforts to confront morally bankrupt laws and practices.

He continued his crusade as an assertive and eloquent defender of civil rights — for everyone — for 24 years as a Supreme Court justice.

The result has not been a perfect society, but Marshall's work has created opportunities his contemporaries could only have dreamed about when he began his historic mission.

Abel Wolman, father of clean water

Sanitary engineer: His 75-year career led
to better health for millions around the world

EACH DAY, MILLIONS of people across the world drink water from faucets and don't think twice about its purity because of a simple chemical process Abel Wolman developed with a classmate in 1918, three years after they graduated from college.

They added small, measured amounts of chlorine, an otherwise toxic substance, to drinking water to kill microorganisms that cause life-threatening diseases.

This celebrated discovery, which dramatically cut disease and improved world health, marked the beginning of an extraordinary career in environmental engineering and public health.

For nearly 75 years, as a sanitary engineer, scientific researcher, Johns Hopkins University professor, consultant and adviser to governments here and abroad, Wolman's work made the world a healthier and more livable place.

The quick disappearance of typhoid as a major killer in Maryland illustrates the magnitude of his early discovery.

Typhoid fever was a common disease in Maryland in 1915 when Wolman joined the Maryland Department of Health as an assistant engineer. By 1930 — 12 years after Wolman helped perfect the chlorination technique — typhoid cases had dropped 92 percent. This astounding change was replicated throughout the world.

Wolman's accomplishments did not end there. He had the unique ability to devise narrow and broad solutions to problems.

He was one of the first to understand that technical engineering questions had widespread public health implications. When Wolman was in his early 30s, he simultaneously edited the *Journal of the American Water Works Association* and the *American Journal of Public Health*. As the first chairman of Hopkins' department of sanitary engineering, he received a joint appointment at the School of Public Health and Hygiene.

Wolman had a prodigious intellect and appetite for work. While Maryland's top sanitary engineer during the Depression, he simultaneously chaired the state Planning Commission in charge of ، .pital improvements and served both the Federal Emergency Administration and the Public Works Administration as chief engineer in Delaware and Maryland.

From these posts, he supervised activities as varied as installing kitchen sinks in hospitals, transplanting oysters and overseeing construction of the Gunpowder-Montebello water tunnel, Montebello Filtration Plant, Friendship Airport and Frederick's sewage treatment system.

He also conceived and designed Prettyboy and Liberty reservoirs and the

Susquehanna water tunnel (the "Big Inch").

Until his death in 1989, Wolman served as an unpaid adviser to Baltimore mayors and Maryland governors on public works. He remained a consultant to 50-plus governments overseas.

Long before the nation's environmental movement, Wolman studied the pollution of rivers, lakes and estuaries.

Under his direction, Maryland became a leader in integrating conventional sanitary engineering with wildlife, recreation and public works construction. He brought this same perspective to the national level, heading the Water Resources Committee of the National Resources Board in 1935.

As part of the U.S. delegation that set up the World Health Organization, Wolman made sure environmental health was an important component of WHO's mission. He was one of the first engineers to push the Atomic Energy Commission to focus on the public-health implications of nuclear power.

Perhaps Wolman's most lasting influence was through his teaching. By 1937, when he received his joint appointment at Johns Hopkins and the School of Public Health and Hygiene, Wolman had already influenced one generation of students. By the time he died in 1989, he had instructed thousands of others who spread his wisdom worldwide.

As dedicated as Abel Wolman was to creating pure water, he understood the world was an imperfect place.

"The belief that cleanliness is an absolute rather than a relative concept makes the health officer's lot not a happy one," he said. "Life in a sterile environment — whether physical, chemical, biological or psychological — is both improbable and undesirable."

Albert C. Ritchie, State House titan

Four-term governor: He dominated state politics
and made Maryland government a model

NO POLITICIAN BEFORE or since has dominated the Maryland political stage the way Albert C. Ritchie did over a 20-year period after World War I. He modernized state government so effectively that the Ritchie model is still in use today.

No Marylander has been a serious presidential candidate — except Ritchie, who did it twice. No Marylander has been elected governor more than two terms — except Ritchie, who did it four times.

Here's a measure of his popularity: At Ritchie's funeral in 1936, 31,000 people filed past the bier as his body lay in state for 24 hours; 1,000 guests jammed Christ Episcopal Church in downtown Baltimore, while 10,000 more stood outside; thousands lined the route to Greenmount Cemetery, where another 10,000 people had gathered.

His death at age 59 was a national loss, wrote the *New York Herald Tribune*. The *Washington Post* eulogized Ritchie as a man of "courage, honesty, realism and intelligence." The *New York Times* called him "an administrator of large ability" who "made his state an example of good government... He had the strength of his convictions."

H. L. Mencken praised Ritchie's "extraordinary capacity for public administration" and his "immense skill at simplifying complicated and confusing problems, and a high degree of courage in resolving them."

Albert Cabell Ritchie, the scion of old Virginia and Maryland families, brought Maryland into the progressive era.

As a Baltimore lawyer, he pioneered the use of litigation to win lower gas and electricity rates. His fame made him an easy winner in 1915 as state attorney general, an office he revamped before taking time off to work as a protege to financier Bernard M. Baruch on the War Industries Board in Washington.

In 1919, he won his first term as governor by 165 votes, surviving a year of Republicans sweeps. The next three times, he was elected by landslides.

Ritchie created a statewide organization that was rarely challenged. His agenda proved enlightened and far-sighted.

He cut the size of state government from 85 agencies to 19 departments, implemented executive budgeting, put in place a merit system, simplified a profusion of state and local elections and set up a Central Purchasing Bureau.

Ritchie monitored expenses zealously, using the savings for tax cuts as well as for more roads, better facilities for the mentally ill and wayward juveniles and a broader workers compensation law.

Maryland's public schools, ranked among the nation's worst, were revamped. Ritchie tossed out inept school superintendents, raised teacher salaries and focused on secondary education — unheard of back then. He was the first Maryland governor — but not the last — to create an equaliza- tion fund to help poorer school systems.

Yet Ritchie was a fervent conservative. He rose to national prominence in the 1920s defending states' rights. He felt that states were in far better posi- tion to handle social problems than the federal bureaucracy. Eighty years later, this remains a bedrock belief of conservatives.

He led the crusade against Prohibition, not because he loved liquor but because he didn't want Washington dictating to governors. Maryland, he told a succession of presidents, was perfectly capable of handling a coal strike, child labor abuses or the need for more education funds.

Twice his forthright conservatism made him a presidential contender. Franklin D. Roosevelt's campaign manager offered Ritchie the vice presi- dential spot in 1932, but Ritchie wisely rejected it because of the yawning philosophical gulf between himself and FDR. He proved to be a stern Roosevelt critic.

The Depression, the popularity of the New Deal and the public's unease with a governor already 15 years in office led to Ritchie's defeat in 1934.

By then, his greatest contributions had long been achieved. Marylanders are still benefiting from the government reforms and health and education programs advanced by Albert Ritchie.

Eubie Blake, musician for the ages

Songwriter, pianist: In early 1900s, he helped
establish ragtime as a major jazz precursor

"IF I'D KNOWN I was gonna live this long, I'd have taken better care of myself," Eubie Blake remarked while celebrating his 100th birthday.

Sadly, if he hadn't lived until he was 100, James Herbert "Eubie" Blake wouldn't be the household name he is. What a shame if younger people had missed the pleasure that his music brings.

"Love Will Find a Way." "Memories of You." "I'm Just Wild About Harry" (Harry Truman's presidential campaign song in 1948). Those were among the 300 songs he wrote.

The revival of ragtime in the late 1960s and 1970s, with its syncopated rhythms and feel-good quality, brought Blake out of retirement.

"You see, people forgot about me for a while," he told a reporter for *The Sun*, "and they forgot about ragtime music until they did that Scott Joplin tune 'The Entertainer' in [the movie] 'The Sting.' All of a sudden ragtime was back in style and I was the only original ragtime pianist still alive."

Born in Baltimore in 1883 and reared at 319 Forrest Street, Blake was the youngest of 11 children and the only one to survive infancy. He was the son of former slaves.

"I'm proud of my heritage," he once said. "I want everyone to know I came from slavery and went to the top of my profession." His father, John Sumner Blake, was a longshoreman who had fought in the Union Army. His mother, Emily Johnston Blake, was a laundress.

Blake attended the segregated Primary School No. 2 in the 200 block of East Street. "I got kicked out in the eighth grade for something — I don't have to lie now — I didn't do," Blake told a *Sun* reporter in the early 1970s.

At a young age, Blake taught himself by ear to play the family's pump organ. He later took formal music lessons, learning to play the cornet as well as the piano.

To the dismay of his mother, he became interested in ragtime, in which the right hand plays syncopated, or ragged, rhythms while the left hand keeps a steady beat. Without her knowledge, he began playing ragtime piano in bars and other venues of which she would not have approved, launching at the age of 15 a professional career that — with interruptions — lasted until his death 85 years later, in 1983.

High points included his collaboration with singer and lyricist Noble Sissle. Together, they performed in vaudeville in the United States and Europe. The first song they wrote together, "It's All Your Fault" was performed by headliner Sophie Tucker.

In 1921, the two men teamed up to bring to Broadway the first black musical comedy, "Shuffle Along." Among the cast members were Florence Mills,

Paul Robeson and — in the chorus — Josephine Baker.

Four other Blake musicals followed before his attempted retirement in the 1940s. He began to tour with the USO during World War II and make other appearances, but he later slipped into relative obscurity with the continuing decline of ragtime.

That period of obscurity ended in the 1960s.

Blake made a comeback that included recordings, concerts and television appearances, exposing another generation to ragtime and his infectious spirit.

He was awarded honorary degrees and other accolades. In 1978, his life and music were celebrated in the Broadway show, "Eubie," which was later televised in the United States and staged in London.

Again, the irrepressible Eubie Blake — as well as his music — proved an international sensation.

Claire McCardell and the American look

Designer: At a time when the fashion world looked to Paris, this Frederick native looked away

SHE HAS BEEN called a revolutionary and a liberator. Yet few today know the name Claire McCardell.

Walk into a department store, though, and "McCardellisms" fill the racks — in pedal pushers, wraparound dresses, hoods, spaghetti straps and revealing swimwear. McCardell, a Frederick native, was author of the "American look" for women.

She was born in 1905 and showed her fancy for fashion early, making paper dolls from women's magazine photos and designing her dresses with the help of the family's seamstress. After graduating from high school, she spent two years in the home economics program at Hood College before persuading her parents to let her study at the School of Fine and Applied Arts (later Parsons School of Design) in New York.

The fashion world McCardell entered in 1926 was fixated on Paris, where she completed course work and copied couture. She and schoolmates combed flea markets, buying French clothes and bringing them back to their rooms to unstitch their secrets.

With a head full of ideas, McCardell returned to New York and graduated from Parsons. She then spent three frustrating years getting hired and fired, painting lamp shades and modeling before meeting designer Robert Turk, who took her with him in 1929 to Townley Frocks, a dress and sportswear company. Three years later, after Turk's death in a boating accident, McCardell, then just 27, was asked to finish his fall line.

An avid athlete, McCardell designed clothes for active women. Her mass-produced, affordable fashions were revolutionary in their spareness, their nod to menswear and use of "experimental" fabrics like jersey and rayon.

For several years, reviews of her radical designs were spotty. Her breakthrough came in 1938, when after several years of working with different designers, she returned to Townley and created the "Monastic" dress, which drew on Algerian styling and hung simply from the shoulders and could be belted any way by the wearer. This success gained her the right to put the McCardell name on her clothes, a recognition few designers of the time achieved.

During World War II, McCardell stepped into the design void left after the Nazis dropped the curtain on French fashion. She took government surpluses of weather balloon cottons and turned them into sportswear; in 1942, she came out with the $6.95 Popover, a stylish wraparound denim dress, with a matching oven mitt, for busy housewives.

McCardell became a sensation.

She was a regular visitor to Maryland during these years, coming home to ski or visit family. She was married in 1943 at St. Paul's Episcopal Church in Baltimore to Texas architect Irving Harris. Twice a year, she passed along new designs to an aunt, Pauline McCardell, who lived in Frederick and became the hometown purveyor of her niece's clothes.

After the war, she turned to helping aspiring designers as a volunteer critic in the fashion design department at Parsons. She also worked on an advisory panel formed by Time Inc. in 1954 to create a new magazine, from which *Sports Illustrated* was born.

The award-winning designer's star was still rising in the 1950s when she was diagnosed with cancer. In January 1958, just two months before her death at 52, McCardell slipped out of the hospital with her former schoolmate and design collaborator, Mildred Orrick, to attend her last show.

Claire McCardell was a mother of modernism. She was also a shy, small-town Maryland girl who parlayed paper dolls into party dresses, followed her dreams to the big time — and made it.

Her work remains quite visible, not only in the Victoria and Albert Museum in London, the Fashion Institute of Technology in New York, and the Maryland Historical Society in Baltimore, but in racks of women's wear in stores throughout the world.

Harry Kelley, bullish on the beach

Ocean City mayor: One of state's most
colorful politicians, he led resort into a vibrant era

CROSSING THE Mason-Dixon Line from Delaware into Maryland, the shimmering blue water to your left is the Atlantic Ocean.

Harry Kelley did not create that.

But continue south into Ocean City and you pass landmarks that Kelley, mayor from 1970 from 1985, influenced immensely. It probably took 20 minutes to travel this barrier island when Kelley entered politics in the 1960s. With all the congestion, traffic signals, shops and restaurants, it can take four times that long now.

Ocean City has had only five mayors. Harry William Kelley Jr. was the third, and the most prolific. His tenure belongs on the short list of events — the storms of 1933 and 1962, the boom of sportfishing and the Bay Bridge — that transformed this corner of the Eastern Shore.

Kelley's paneled office was adorned with a photograph of his political hero, Mayor Richard J. Daley of Chicago. But the unpolished manner of "Ol' Kell," his media theatrics and fierce hometown loyalty were reminiscent of another big-city mayor closer to home: William Donald Schaefer.

Kelley led by gut instinct. During the oil embargo, he posed before a convoy of gasoline tankers, promising vacationers he'd fill their cars to get them home. Another time, he mounted a bulldozer, defying authorities who had nixed his plan to rebuild the jetties.

Today, the Ocean City beachfront is free and open to the public. Kelley insisted it remain so. Let other resorts carve niche markets for the rich, college students or retirees. Ocean City covets a family-oriented middle market. Because of this, it has staying power.

When Kelley took over as mayor, the resort was host to fewer than 200,000 visitors on summer weekends and 11,000 in the winter. Today, weekend visits are up to 300,000 in summer, 75,000 in winter. Last summer, the city recorded 4.3 million visits.

As you continue south, near 120th Street stands a fortress of condominiums up to 27 stories tall. Kelley lobbied for these behemoths, which distinguish Ocean City from the mostly low-rise coastal development from Delaware to the Carolinas. No condo units were built in Ocean City in 1966; almost 7,000 rose in 1972-1973.

This "Gold Coast" smacks of excess to some, but the towers' vast worth made possible the town's conservative, pay-as-you-go financing. The assessable tax base vaulted from $100 million when Kelley was first elected to $600 million when he died in office at age 66. It's $1.3 billion now.

"When Harry took over, he literally had a city with no infrastructure whatsoever. The police were untrained and wore ragged uniforms," recalled

Warren Frame, a hotelier who served with Kelley on the town council. "He led us to being a first-class city."

Continue to 40th Street. On your right is the Ocean City Convention Center, fresh from a $30 million expansion. Kelley promoted the original $4 million project. Raised in his family's seaside hotel, Kelley recognized that Ocean City needed to extend its season.

Another dozen blocks south the boardwalk begins, with the smell of sea salt, french fries and warm caramel corn. It has been a major draw since the turn of the century, when town fathers laid out the planks each morning and retrieved them each night.

About the only entity not vying for your money is a slot machine. Every mayor before and since Kelley has fought legalized gambling. But his highly vocal opposition was crucial, coming as Atlantic City, N.J., plunged into casinos.

On to Third Street and City Hall, site of many Kelley wins — and a stiff repudiation. In 1981, the council, fed up with his headstrong style, hired a full-time manager to run the city. Yet even in defeat, including his ill-fated campaign for governor in 1982, Kelley gained publicity for his town.

"I've learned just how much Elvis and Harry Kelley have in common," current Mayor James N. Mathias said. "They both live forever."

To leave the town, take U.S. 50 over Sinepuxent Bay, busy with charter boats and jet skiers. You can't avoid a final reminder of the man who helped make Ocean City when you cross the Harry Kelley Memorial Bridge.

James Rouse shaped our cities

Builder: Harborplace and Columbia
are among the many grand projects he developed

CAN YOU IMAGINE Baltimore without Harborplace? Or the Baltimore-Washington corridor without the vibrant community of Columbia? Or the nation without enclosed shopping malls that are America's new Main Street?

A half-century ago, none of those projects were on our radar screen. The vision, business acumen and salesmanship of James Wilson Rouse, the Eastern Shore-born developer extraordinaire, put all these landmarks on the map.

Rouse thought on a grand scale. And because his ideas bore fruit, he became the country's most important real estate developer in the second half of the 20th century.

He turned a tiny Baltimore real-estate financing office into a powerhouse developer of urban and suburban shopping centers. Locally, he built the city's first shopping mall, Mondawmin, and the region's first enclosed mall, Harundale. His Village of Cross Keys remains an idyllic urban community.

Along the way, he gained national prominence. President Eisenhower named him to his Advisory Committee on Housing. He chaired its subcommittee on urban redevelopment, rehabilitation and conservation. Four decades later, President Clinton awarded him the Medal of Freedom.

He made the cover of *Time* magazine. "Cities are Fun!" it proclaimed. This phrase captured his optimism for urban life, whether for cities as old as Baltimore or as new as Columbia.

As a real estate developer, he etched his signature on more than 100 city centers on five continents.

Rouse led the drive to rescue the Inner Harbor, first as chairman of the Greater Baltimore Committee and then as head of the Rouse Co. He restored Boston's Faneuil Hall Marketplace in Boston, built Gallery at Market East in downtown Philadelphia, South Street Seaport in New York and numerous similar urban marketplaces.

He had a knack for catchy phrases to promote his projects: He is credited with coining the terms "shopping mall" and "urban renewal." Most of his developments remain prime attractions.

It would be fair to compare him to architects who shaped London, Paris and Vienna, or to Frank Lloyd Wright and Frederick Law Olmsted or even to Walt Disney.

Like all of them, Rouse could look at a vast expanse and dream wildly. The Inner Harbor consisted of rundown wharves before he envisioned a new Baltimore.

Before he turned his attention to a 14,000-acre area between Baltimore and Washington, most people saw farmland. Rouse dreamed of a new city, bustling with 100,000 residents, a strong business base and a new concept of racial and socioeconomic harmony.

Columbia is 32 years old and close to buildout. It has lost some of the idealism he championed, but the quality of life, strong economic base and anti-sprawl planning have made it a hit.

Jim Rouse was first and foremost a businessman. His companies built an impressive financial track record. But making money was never his only reason for work.

Long before we heard the phrase "compassionate conservative," Rouse showed that a businessman could have a big heart. His fight against poverty and urban blight dates to the early 1950s.

"He was disdainful of people in business who were not committed to improving the human condition," former Rouse Co. lawyer George Barker said after Rouse's death in 1996. "He believed that you could do that and still make a profit."

Rouse remained a general in the war on poverty. His Enterprise Foundation formed a partnership with City Hall to help the poor find jobs, build decent housing for them and provide health care in the Sandtown-Winchester neighborhood. The foundation is duplicating that effort elsewhere.

In spite of his success and drive, Rouse remained humble, favoring madras sports jackets, penny loafers and his trusty, dated Buick.

Giving cities renewed vitality — and conquering social ills — were key Rouse objectives. Giving suburbs a more human and cosmopolitan face were also priorities. James Rouse's vision has become America's vision.

Lillie Carroll Jackson, mother of a movement

Mitchell matriarch: Through NAACP, she
helped secure civil rights in Maryland

WHEN TWO MARYLAND colleges refused to admit Lillie Carroll Jackson's two oldest daughters because of their race, she packed them off to schools in New York and Pennsylvania.

For her it was just another in a series of slights and insults she had to endure as an African-American living under Jim Crow segregation rules. But she didn't take her plight sitting down: Instead, the former school teacher organized black Baltimoreans to protest everything from Eastern Shore lynchings to the discriminatory practices of local retailers. Eventually, whites joined her protests, too.

Many people credit her tireless work as president of the Baltimore and Maryland branches of the NAACP as helping to establish a model of activism for the modern civil rights movement, which has resulted in today's burgeoning black middle class.

It's somehow fitting that Jackson, as a descendant of Charles Carroll, a signer of the Declaration of Independence, would confront an unjust government, asking it to fulfill its creed that all men are created equal.

Galvanized by the 1933 Eastern Shore lynching of a black man, Jackson joined *Afro-American* editor Carl J. Murphy in organizing a series of successful protests to help put an end to such lawlessness. The demonstrations evolved into a campaign for economic and social justice, including the "Buy Where You Can Work" boycott against white merchants.

Three days after that protest began, an A&P grocery store in Northwest Baltimore negotiated a settlement that included hiring black employees. Word of this success spread around the nation, prompting similar boycotts in other cities.

Jackson was a spitfire of a woman who had known much adversity in her life. A botched surgery to repair damaged nerve tissue while she was in her 20s left her face contorted. Yet her shrill voice demanded attention. She was known for marathon telephone calls.

The late Baltimore mayor and Maryland governor Theodore R. McKeldin, eager to avoid a Jackson call, is said to have once told an assistant who was on the telephone with the assertive civil rights leader, "I'd rather the devil got after me than Mrs. Jackson. Give her what she wants."

In his biography of Supreme Court Justice Thurgood Marshall, author Juan Williams wrote that as a young pro bono lawyer for the Baltimore NAACP, Marshall would often lay the telephone receiver on his desk while Lillie Jackson dictated strategy. He would occasionally say a word or two to let her know he hadn't hung up.

But her persistance paid off. She prompted many elected officials to act.

Jackson and others helped Marshall develop legal strategies that he eventually took to the national stage.

Jackson was president of the Baltimore branch of the NAACP an astounding 35 years, from 1935 to 1970. She took it from a handful of members to its peak of more than 18,000 in 1946. She served in the same capacity with the NAACP's state branch for 20 years after its founding in 1942. She died in 1975 at age 86.

She was matriarch of the politically active Mitchell clan that has included her son-in-law, the late Clarence Mitchell Jr., who was so influential as the chief NAACP Washington lobbyist that he was known as "the 101st senator"; her daughter (and Clarence Mitchell's wife), the late Juanita Jackson Mitchell, a lawyer who led the battle for civil rights in the NAACP and in state and local courts; her brother-in-law, retired U.S. Rep. Parren J. Mitchell; and several grandchildren and great-grandchildren who have held elective office.

The successful struggle for civil rights in Maryland was a defining achievement of this century. Lillie Carroll Jackson was a key general in that battle.

William Preston Lane: He unified the state

Bay Bridge champion: Governor ended
Eastern Shore's isolation from rest of Maryland

WHEN IT COMES to courage, William Preston Lane Jr. could teach today's Maryland politicians a lesson. He often put his career on the line to do the right thing. Achievements mattered, not longevity in office.

In the 1930s, then-Attorney General Lane sent in state troopers and the National Guard to find the perpetrators of two lynchings on the Eastern Shore. He was warned it could end his career, but he persisted because he abhorred intolerance and discrimination.

His car was stoned, he was vilified, but Lane persisted, even testifying before Congress. He became a national hero and helped turn the tide of opinion against lynchings. But it cost him any chance for re-election in 1934.

A decade later, then Governor Lane — again warned of the political dangers — rammed through the state's first sales tax. In the wake of skimpy wartime budgets, Maryland's infrastructure was in deplorable shape. He vowed to change that.

Lane's postwar modernization succeeded, but he was cast in the role of tax villain.

Today, Pres Lane is best remembered for another courageous act — overcoming 45 years of opposition to a bridge spanning the Chesapeake Bay. That achievement transformed life on the Eastern Shore, ended its dependence on Wilmington and Philadelphia and sparked a booming vacation and tourist trade in Ocean City.

The 4.2-mile-long, $45 million bridge ranks not only as an engineering marvel but as the most important public works project in state history. It literally opened the Eastern Shore — a sleepy, backwater vestige of the Deep South — to the 20th century. The man who made it happen was born into Hagerstown's most prominent family. He married Dorothy Byron, daughter of the town's second-most important family, and wound up running the town newspaper, a bank, a law firm and a shoe factory.

He returned from World War I a decorated hero and enlisted in the cadre of Gov. Albert C. Ritchie. Within a few years, Lane had firm political control as a ward heeler of Washington County.

He, along with William C. Walsh in Allegany and Garrett counties, David C. Winebrenner in Frederick County and E. Brooke Lee in Montgomery County, were dubbed Ritchie's "knights of the west." They directed their counties' political fortunes for three decades.

In his one term as governor, Lane produced prodigious changes. By forcing through a reluctant legislature not only a new sales tax but higher levies on existing taxes, Lane paved the way for major spending projects.

Lane's state budget increased 25 percent each year. A fast-expanding

University of Maryland accommodated a wave of returning veterans on the G.I. bill; elementary schools were built to prepare for the postwar "baby boom."

Farmers, businessmen and new suburbanites demanded better transportation, which Lane set in motion with 1,110 miles of new roads, including the Baltimore-Washington Parkway and the Annapolis-Washington Parkway (U.S. 50).

When *The Sun* ran a Pulitzer Prize-winning series on the mistreatment of the mentally ill, Lane responded with new hospitals not only for citizens with psychiatric problems (Spring Grove) but for those with mental retardation (Rosewood) and tuberculosis (Mount Wilson).

In the end, none of these good deeds mattered to voters. They dubbed the governor's sales tax "Pennies for Lane." He was nearly defeated in a vicious Democratic primary, then soundly trounced in the 1950 general election.

Two years later, though, Lane helped christen the Chesapeake Bay Bridge. The original span still carries his name. Millions traverse it every year. It has spurred commerce and unified citizens on both shores of the Chesapeake. It remains William Preston Lane Jr.'s greatest achievement.

Charles P. McCormick, populist employer

Spice merchant: Golden Rule was the basis
for his successful technique for managing people

CHARLES P. MCCORMICK was a revolutionary in a business suit.

When he took over the family's Baltimore spice and extract business in 1932, he decided to treat employees as if they were partners. Colleagues thought he was out of his mind. Standard management practice of the day was to view workers as machines — to be run until they broke down.

At the height of the Depression, C. P. McCormick startled the local business community. While others were cutting pay and laying off employees, he handed workers a 10 percent raise and shortened the work week from 56 to 46 hours. He also promised to end the three annual seasonal layoffs his late uncle, Willoughby McCormick, had favored as a cost-cutting measure.

The conventional wisdom was that C. P., as his employees called him, would run the money-losing business into the ground. But instead of reporting another year of red ink, the company moved into the black — during the Depression. For the three decades C. P. ran the firm, McCormick & Co. prospered.

Charles Perry McCormick was born in 1896, the son of Baptist missionaries in Mexico. He spent much time in countries that were suspicious of or hostile to democracy and capitalism. When he came to the United States for schooling as a teen, he developed a profound appreciation for freedom and free enterprise — and the Golden Rule.

His first McCormick job was sweeping floors on school vacations. After attending Johns Hopkins University and serving in the Navy, C. P. joined the company in 1919 as a salesman and then a sales supervisor for McCormick's patent medicines in the South. By 1926, he had joined the board.

From these posts, he studied the business acumen of his uncle, Willoughby, who over 30 years built a small distributor of spices and extracts into an international enterprise by stressing quality. (Willoughby created the slogan "Make the best — someone will buy it.")

C. P., however, was convinced his uncle's management style hurt performance. "My uncle ruled with as firm a hand as he had in the one-room factory," C. P. wrote.

He was convinced the company's continuing losses stemmed from poor employee morale and low productivity. He believed McCormick workers had more to contribute than their sweat. This notion formed the foundation for his "multiple management" method.

Shortly after cutting hours and raising pay, C. P. asked 17 young executives to form a junior board of directors to provide new ideas.

This experiment proved so successful that within a year C. P. formed a board of factory workers. It made recommendations to improve manufacturing processes, cut costs and increase profits.

C. P. noted a changed attitude. "They began to show that poise and thoughtfulness which distinguishes all men when they realize their responsibility to their fellows and share the obligations of the success of a business," he wrote. C. P. also created a sales board. He brought women and blacks into management long before the advent of affirmative action.

In the 1940s, other national companies embraced C. P.'s multiple-management style. But many executives did not subscribe to his methods. C. P. "Buzz" McCormick Jr., his son, recalls that his father joined the board of the National Association of Manufacturers but soon was asked to leave. "Some of them considered my father to be a Communist," his son says with a chuckle.

Long before the term was coined, C. P. believed in "community service." One day each year, McCormick employees worked on an off-day and donated their earnings to the Baltimore Community Chest. This practice, called C-Day, began in 1941 and continues today in all of McCormick's divisions.

C. P., who played football at school but was never a star, also established a prestigious annual award for the "unsung heroes" of Maryland high school football.

In an editorial written after his death in July 1970, *The Sun* pointed out that C. P. McCormick was a man who "bartered in teas, spices and humanity, who lived his ideals to the full by his word and, even more abundantly, by his example."

Theodore R. McKeldin modernized Maryland

Governor and mayor: Baltimorean envisioned
today's airport and Inner Harbor, practiced racial equality

LEGACIES OF THEODORE Roosevelt McKeldin, Maryland's pre-eminent political leader after World War II, are all around us: In his two terms as governor and two terms as Baltimore mayor, he built what today is the Baltimore-Washington International Airport, started the Inner Harbor rebirth and oversaw a massive highway program that included the Baltimore and Washington beltways and the first car tunnel under the Patapsco River.

Equally important was the civility and moderate tone this Republican set for the overwhelmingly Democratic state. In words and deeds, he promoted racial equality, a stand that led to his exclusion from the Southern Governors Conference. But, then, McKeldin was a man of principle and strong convictions.

Even though he had won prominence at the 1952 Republican National Convention by making a stirring nominating speech for Dwight D. Eisenhower, 12 years later McKeldin rejected the GOP's choice of Barry M. Goldwater, throwing his support behind Democratic President Lyndon B. Johnson.

So important was McKeldin's backing that Johnson helicoptered to Baltimore to thank him. After the election, the president made federal funds available to start the Inner Harbor revitalization.

Remarkably, 25 years after McKeldin's death at 73, dozens of aging Republicans and Democrats around the state look back to their time with him as defining moments. Veteran real estate agent James Crockett, who worked for McKeldin in Baltimore's African-American neighborhoods, noted, "If he told you something, you could depend on that. He never disappointed you."

Little in McKeldin's early life suggested he was destined for greatness. The tenth of 11 children, he was born to an illiterate South Baltimore stonecutter so fond of drink that Teddy swore off liquor forever. At 14, he quit school and took a bank job. Evenings he studied for his high school diploma; on weekends he toiled as a gravedigger, investing his savings in Dale Carnegie speech classes.

At 25, he graduated from the University of Maryland evening law school. He soon put his famous oratorical skills to work for William F. Broening, another Republican who overcame the formidable odds to become Baltimore's mayor.

America was at war when McKeldin himself was first elected mayor in 1943. In 1950, he defeated Democratic incumbent William Preston Lane Jr. to become governor.

He inherited a state undergoing vast, fundamental economic and social changes. During his two terms as governor, suburbanization altered Maryland profoundly, creating unprecedented demands for public spending and services. Equally significant were fundamental social changes, above all the breakdown of Jim Crow laws and racial segregation.

This rapid transformation fueled demagoguery. But McKeldin would have none of that. "The minority groups — they elected me," he proclaimed, appointing blacks, Jews and women to offices they had not occupied before.

Publicly and behind the scenes, he worked to end segregation in Baltimore theaters, stores and lunch counters. As governor, he ordered the integration of state ferries and beaches, abolished racially based lists for state jobs and played a crucial role in ending school and hotel segregation.

By 1963, when he was elected mayor of Baltimore for the second time, the nation was in the midst of its civil rights struggle. Open accommodations and fair employment became sensitive local issues. In 1966, when the Congress on Racial Equality held its convention here and announced Baltimore as its target city for the next year, McKeldin addressed the group, embraced its goals and promised full cooperation.

"McKeldin was ahead of his time," said Peter Marudas, who left *The Evening Sun* to become the mayor's chief of staff during those years. "He always practiced the politics of inclusion."

Jacob Blaustein created an oil empire

Amoco founder: He built a global giant, helped launch
Charles Center and served as U.S. diplomat

JACOB BLAUSTEIN STARTED a vast oil marketing empire with a horse and a wagon.

In 1910, 18-year-old Jacob and his father, Louis, formed the impressive-sounding American Oil Co. and sold kerosene in Baltimore from a horse-drawn tank wagon.

American Oil — now part of the petroleum colossus BP Amoco, formed in 1998 when British Petroleum acquired Amoco — first operated out of a livery stable on Clarkson and Wells streets. The family horse, Prince, pulled a wagon with a large metal tank.

Louis, who fled Lithuania in 1888, sold petroleum products for John D. Rockefeller's Standard Oil of New Jersey for 18 years. But it was Jacob who shaped the enterprise's destiny.

He studied chemistry in college but left to help his father. The son devised better refining methods and cleaner-burning kerosene. Soon the Blausteins were far out-selling competitors.

Jacob Blaustein was instrumental in creating anti-knock, high-octane motor fuel for high-compression engines that were so popular with early auto designers and manufacturers. His company came up with two market-ing breakthroughs — the drive-through filling station and the metered pump.

At Amoco's first retail outlet on Cathedral Street, the Lord Baltimore Filling Station, motorists could pull off the street to put gasoline in their cars. Until then, cars were fueled at the curb — a messy and clumsy process.

Early pumps lacked any metering system. The Blausteins' pumps were topped with a 10-gallon glass jar and gallon markings on the side. Amoco's slogan: "See what you get, and get what you see."

As automobiles grew in importance, Jacob Blaustein turned Amoco into a global giant. American Oil Co. became a subsidiary of Standard Oil of Indiana in 1954.

It was only one arm of the family's operations. The Blausteins' American Trading and Production Co. held interests in ocean tankers, manufacturing, banking, insurance and real estate companies, as well as a controlling share of Crown Central Petroleum.

Jacob Blaustein played an important role in downtown Baltimore's revival. After a selection committee rejected his proposal for a skyscraper at One Charles Center in favor of a Mies van der Rohe-designed tower, Blaustein bought the Hub Department Store across the street. He knocked it down and built his own 30-story structure, one story taller than One Charles Center. His bold decision spurred additional office development.

Blaustein was more than an entrepreneur. He advised five presidents and undertook diplomatic missions to Germany, Israel, North Africa, South America and the United Nations.

In 1945, President Franklin D. Roosevelt asked Blaustein to attend the formative meetings of the United Nations. Through his efforts, the U.N. charter included language on basic human rights.

Although he was not a Zionist, Blaustein played a key role in cementing U.S.-Israeli relations. His close ties with David Ben-Gurion, Israel's first prime minister, led to an accord on the status of American Jews and Israel known as the Ben-Gurion/Blaustein Agreements.

After World War II, he negotiated payments of hundreds of millions of dollars to victims of the Nazis. In 1960, he helped get the German industrial conglomerate Krupp to make cash payments to slave laborers who had worked in its munitions plant. Current negotiations with German companies to reimburse other victims of Nazi forced-labor policies are based on this precedent-setting arrangement.

Blaustein's philanthropy extended to the Baltimore Symphony Orchestra and The Associated Jewish Charities. The Jacob and Hilda Blaustein Foundation supports a range of programs — from religious pluralism in Israel to cutting-edge research at the Johns Hopkins Wilmer Eye Institute.

Jacob Blaustein died in 1970. Baltimoreans, whether they are filling their cars with gasoline or listening to the BSO performing a Mozart concerto, are the beneficiaries of this remarkable but unpretentious man's legacy.

Babe Ruth's legend lives on

American icon: Baltimore was the house that built Ruth, the slugger who invented sports celebrity

BABE RUTH'S IMPACT is difficult to describe: It was too Ruthian.

He rescued and reinvented baseball as the American pastime. He was the prime reason for the first palatial baseball stadium. He was the first player represented by an agent — and we know where that's led.

George Herman Ruth, born in a West Baltimore row house, redefined celebrity. He was without question the best-known American personality in the years between the two world wars — and remains high on nearly everyone's list to this day.

Like John Wayne, Elvis Presley and Marilyn Monroe, his image represented America to the world. Japanese soldiers cursed his name, believing that would offend U.S. troops in World War II. Though some of Ruth's greatest baseball records have been eclipsed, no athlete has achieved such prolonged international fame.

Most people link the swashbuckling slugger to the New York Yankees, his team from 1920 to 1934. He also played seven years for Boston as a superb pitcher.

But if Yankee Stadium was the House that Ruth Built, Baltimore was the house that built Ruth.

Had Xaverian brother Matthias Boutilier not recognized Ruth's baseball prowess at the St. Mary's Industrial School for Boys, the lad might have been a shirtmaker or bartender like his dad.

One of the Ruth family's homes was located in today's Camden Yards outfield. George was shoplifting at age 5, chewing tobacco at 7. His parents sent him to live at the reform school because they couldn't control him.

His world was confined to Southwest Baltimore. When he left Maryland in his late teens on road trips as a member of the minor-league Baltimore Orioles in 1914, he rode a train for the first time and bribed a hotel elevator operator so he could joy ride up and down.

Ruth revolutionized the game, striking a baseball with a ferocity never seen. He hit more home runs than entire teams. He bashed one in Detroit 602 feet — 100 feet farther than the homer hit by Mark McGwire in 1999 that had the baseball world agog.

Others are still judged against Ruth's standards. His season record of 60 home runs and his career total of 714 were untouched for nearly two generations. He still holds most of baseball's slugging records. Opponents moved back their outfield fences to compensate. The Yankees built an immense stadium to suit not just Ruth's home-run hitting, but his magnetic gate appeal.

His rise came at a lucky time for baseball. A controversy over players fixing the 1919 World Series soured the public just as Ruth became a Yankee.

He helped cleanse the stain of the "Black Sox scandal," just as Cal Ripken's consecutive-games streak helped baseball recover popularity after a players' strike 75 years later.

Nothing in modern sports compares with the Ruth phenomenon. His exploits — even his high jinks — on and off the field assumed almost mythic status.

His popularity far surpassed presidents and entertainers. His devotion to children, his charitable work on their behalf after he retired, his zest for life and his boyish devotion to a game that captured America's heart made him a legend in his own time.

When Ruth died of cancer at age 53 in 1948, 75,000 mourners ringed Yankee Stadium where his body lay in state. His image remains marketable, even overseas: A chain of Babe Ruth restaurants thrives in London today. Baltimore, where he was born, raised and started his career, opened a museum to celebrate his achievements.

The endurance of his appeal defies explanation. He had a peculiar shape, a bulldog's face and a personal life of excesses as confused as any of today's superstars. But from the Roaring Twenties through the Depression, he made Americans feel good about themselves. He still does.

Helen Taussig, pioneer cardiologist

'Blue babies': Hopkins physician's breakthrough
work created pediatric heart surgery

FOR Helen Brooke Taussig, it was a lifetime affair of the heart. Through her scientific vision and human compassion, thousands of gasping "blue babies" once condemned to an early death or severe invalidism gained a new life.

The Johns Hopkins pediatric cardiologist conceived of an operation to repair heart birth defects in children whose blood was starved of oxygen, turning their skin a bluish hue.

The historic 1944 operation connected a major artery out of the heart to the artery going into the lungs, increasing the vital supply of oxygen to the blood. That medical breakthrough at Johns Hopkins laid the foundation of modern heart surgery.

Taussig was acclaimed by her colleagues as the First Lady of American Medicine, the founder of pediatric cardiology. Hopkins physicians who trained under her demanding tutelage proudly dubbed themselves "the Loyal Knights of Taussig."

But her greatest reward was the enduring love of the children the operation had saved — "my babies," Taussig fondly called them — corresponding with them for decades after their operations. Her scrapbooks chronicled their lives, the patients held regular reunions with her and not a few named their daughters Helen.

"Her fundamental concepts have made possible the modern surgery of the heart, which enables countless children to lead productive lives," read the inscription on the Medal of Freedom, the nation's highest civilian honor, presented to her in 1964 by President Lyndon B. Johnson.

That award came just after she sounded the alarm on dangers of Thalidomide, a popular sedative in Europe.

Alerted by a former pupil, she made a fact-finding tour of West Germany and England and uncovered direct links to horrifying birth defects: children born without limbs, whose mothers had taken the drug during pregnancy. Her reports were instrumental in the U.S. Food and Drug Administration's decision to keep Thalidomide off the domestic market, averting more widespread human tragedy.

She continued to champion tougher new-drug testing, particularly screening for possible birth defects.

Long into official retirement, Taussig continued to investigate rheumatic fever and other childhood ailments of the heart. One-third of her 129 scientific articles were published after retirement from Hopkins in 1963. Her text on congenital heart abnormalities remains a classic in the field.

She was the first woman pediatrics professor at Hopkins, the first woman president of the American Heart Association, the first woman master of the exclusive American College of Physicians. In 1973, she was in the first class of 20 persons inducted into the Women's Hall of Fame.

The tall, intense woman with piercing blue eyes had experienced the prejudice of the male-dominated medical world: denied degree-candidate admission to Harvard in her hometown, receiving full professor rank at Hopkins long after her worldwide acclaim.

Taussig was a redoubtable advocate for female equality in medicine. But acknowledging that men were more likely to become practicing physicians, she fought against gender quotas for medical schools.

Physical hurdles in her life were overcome with characteristic tenacity: dyslexia that hampered her early education reinforced her will to learn; deafness as an adult forced her to use her sensitive hands to "listen" to the patient's heart instead of using a stethoscope; tuberculosis made her keenly aware of the need to help those lacking physical strength.

"Despite her brilliance and prominence, she never lost her simplicity, kindness or compassion," recalled Dr. Denton A. Cooley, the famed heart surgeon and a Taussig pupil.

Even in the impressive pantheon of Johns Hopkins medicine, Helen Brooke Taussig stands out as a rare human being.

Henry Walters' grand art donations

Rail magnate: He collected with passion
and a purpose that became clear only after his death

THE WALTERS ART GALLERY is one of the world's great museums in the breadth and quality of its art of many civilizations. Henry Walters collected with passion, knowledge and wealth, building on the work of his father, William T. Walters.

It was Henry — a secretive man — who collected a museum of the world's culture and then donated it as the heritage of the people of Baltimore.

The gift was unexpected. Henry died at his home in Manhattan, age 83, in 1931. Speculation swirled about the disposition of his art. His will, filed in Baltimore Orphans Court, left the collection of 20,000 objects, the art gallery, the family home at 5 West Mount Vernon Place and one-fourth of his estate as an endowment to the city "for the benefit of the public."

The will set a standard of selfless giving that few donors anywhere have matched.

A. D. Emmart, then *The Sun's* art critic, wrote: "The city has acquired at one stroke an immensely valuable accumulation of paintings and art objects which long since took high rank among the greatest private collections in the country..."

Baltimoreans knew little about their benefactor. Henry was born in 1848 to William T. Walters, a grain and whiskey merchant who collected works of local artists. Having protested the Civil War, William took his family in 1861 to political exile in France. There he expanded his art collecting.

After the war, William Walters returned to Baltimore and restored his fortunes. In 1874, he opened his art-filled home some days, with an admission charge going to charity.

He began collecting small Southern railroads, with a view to uniting them to bring Southern farm produce to northeastern markets. He sent Henry to Georgetown College in Washington, and then Harvard's engineering school.

Henry left in 1889 to manage his father's newly-merged Atlantic Coast Line. He never lived in Baltimore again.

After William Walters died in 1894, Henry moved the railroad's head-quarters to New York. He made annual art-buying trips to Europe, his taste having been formed by the 1870s. He would buy no modern art.

Walters joined the board of the Metropolitan Museum of Art in 1903 and was its second vice president for decades. He joined other wealthy men in subscribing to syndicates that competed in America's Cup ocean yacht races.

All this time, Henry Walters kept his Baltimore ties. He followed his father on the board of the Safe Deposit and Trust Co. (now Mercantile Bankshares Corp.), becoming chairman. He maintained his house, but when visiting stayed in his private rail car.

He gave the Johns Hopkins University a school of medical illustration. He built four public bath houses for the city, serving families that lacked modern plumbing. One still stands on Washington Boulevard.

As he grew older and richer, Walters collected more ambitiously. In 1900, he bought Raphael's "Madonna of the Candelabra" and properties on Charles and Centre streets. In 1902, he bought the huge collection of a Vatican financial official, chartering a steamship to bring it home.

In 1904, he began to build the gallery on his new property to hold his new acquisitions, connected by a bridge to the house he did not inhabit. Architect William Adams Delano modeled the interior on a 17th-century Genoese college and exterior on a 19th-century Parisian mansion. It was finished in 1908.

After Walters' death, the city created a board of trustees and hired a staff, which unpacked crates and spent years learning what it owned. The gallery's doors were opened as a public museum in 1934.

The Walters Art Gallery has been enlarged twice since then and attracted many gifts. Last year, the portion of its $55 million endowment that came from Henry Walters was about $30 million, contributing some $1.5 million of the $11 million budget. Henry Walters is still giving to Baltimore.

E. Brooke Lee's Montgomery County

The Colonel: All politics was local, and foresighted,
when he was the man to see in Washington suburbs

EVERYONE CALLED HIM "The Colonel." Some thought of him as "The Boss." But Edward Brooke Lee was acknowledged as the Founding Father of modern Montgomery County.

A man of energy and vision, Lee was Mr. Democrat in Montgomery when its governmental structure was built and refined. One of the county's principal cities, Silver Spring, took its name from his family's farm.

His lineage included two signers of the Declaration of Independence: Richard Henry Lee and Francis Lightfoot Lee. The Robert E. Lees of Virginia also were part of the family.

Lee's father, Blair, was Maryland's first popularly elected U.S. senator — helped into office by the son's shrewd campaigning.

Brooke Lee left Princeton University without a diploma but got a law degree at George Washington University. When he returned from World War I with a chest full of decorations, the handsome war hero was recruited by Gov. Albert C. Ritchie.

As part of Ritchie's ticket in 1919, Lee was elected state comptroller. Four years later, the governor named him secretary of state. In the next election, he won a House of Delegates seat, then rose rapidly to House speaker in 1927.

All the while he broadened his base in Montgomery, attending to the county's needs in Annapolis and turning out votes as efficiently as any Baltimore ward boss.

His club, Montgomery Democracy, ruled the county with such authority that foes called him a "pint-sized Huey Long." Since Lee stood 6 feet 5 inches, the reference clearly was to Long's demagogic style.

He recognized the importance of helping friends with patronage, his own money and public projects. He even founded his own newspaper, the *Maryland News*, and used it as a platform. Yet Lee proved an unusually prescient political boss.

Realizing his bucolic precincts would be coveted homesites, Lee put in place the county's first zoning and land-use plans. He helped form the Maryland National Parks and Planning Commission and the Washington Suburban Sanitary Commission — key factors in the orderly growth of Prince George's and Montgomery counties.

In addition, the colonel established a championship herd of polled (hornless) Hereford cattle. When his financial fortunes tumbled in the 1940s, he refused to declare bankruptcy, eventually making good on all his debts.

His grip on such a wide swath of Montgomery life did not please everyone. A home-rule charter initiative begun in the 1940s was aimed at ousting him from power, as well as modernizing county government. He defeated the insurgents in 1942 — but his political star was heading downward. He lost his own bid for a seat in Congress that year.

Lee continued to fight the charter because it shifted decision-making from Annapolis, where he retained influence, to the county seat in Rockville. Finally, in 1946, Montgomery voters approved a toned-down revision.

Lee proteges stayed in various public offices into the 1960s. Even in his dotage, the colonel's blessing was sought by aspiring Montgomery candidates. Brooke Lee, who died in 1984 at 91, lived to see his son, Blair Lee III, became lieutenant governor and acting governor.

The colonel built a county of great appeal to the coming generation of suburbanites — including Montgomery's wing of reformers who ironically had made him one of their first targets.

Questions of conflict of interest arose when roads were built, but since Lee was one of the county's largest landholders, new streets and highways inevitably came near his property.

His real estate business was built on what remained of 1,000 acres purchased in the 1800s by his great-grandfather as a summer home at the end of Georgia Avenue. This land is now being developed by a closed family corporation.

E. Brooke Lee was in charge when the county school system was constructed and nurtured. Teacher salaries were set and maintained at the highest level in the state; schools were constructed with the coming growth spurt in mind.

A system of public education that became the best in Maryland, a transportation network, even government reform became part of this patrician boss' proud legacy.

Cal Ripken Jr.'s celebrated work ethic

'Iron Man': An Aberdeen kid grew up to personify
how Maryland likes to view its baseball team — and itself

A SKINNY, BLUE-EYED kid from Aberdeen became an international baseball star — and the most recognizable Marylander of the past quarter-century.

Cal Ripken Jr. is bound to get his 3,000th hit in 2000. That milestone eluded him when injury shortened his 1999 season for the Orioles. But with or without it, his legacy in the great American pastime is as solid as a bronze plaque hanging in the Hall of Fame.

He gained global fame in 1995 when he surpassed a record everyone thought was unreachable: the streak of 2,130 consecutive games played by the New York Yankees' Lou Gehrig in the 1920s and 1930s. For three more years, Ripken continued to defy the wear and tear of a baseball season by playing every game. He ended the streak voluntarily a year ago at 2,632 games.

Though he missed half of the 1999 season when his 39-year-old back betrayed him, he finished as one of the Orioles' hottest hitters.

His ability to play baseball is only part of the story. His evolution as a goodwill ambassador for the game, and for his native state, is even more remarkable.

Calvin Edwin Ripken Jr., after all, was born to play ball. He was a great soccer player as well as a baseball pitcher and shortstop. His father was an Orioles coach. His mother spent a lot of time around the game herself. (When young Cal overheard parents justify to their sons that he had defeated them in Little League because his dad was an Oriole, he would resist the urge to tell them his mother taught him many of the finer points.)

His small-town, sports-oriented upbringing, however, couldn't have prepared him for what he became beyond the diamond: a venerated symbol for the game. That's evident by ovations he receives across the country. It's also proved by another fact: Fans nationwide have elected him to the starting lineup at the annual All Star Game a record 15 straight times.

He has only played for one team — a unique achievement in an era of players jumping to the highest bidder. That he has played in his hometown his whole career is even rarer.

Maryland has been home to many famous athletes this century, including baseball Hall-of-Famers Babe Ruth, Brooks Robinson and Frank Robinson; the boxer Sugar Ray Leonard; football's John Unitas, considered by many the greatest quarterback ever; not to mention the champion thoroughbreds Northern Dancer and Cigar. But Ripken became one of the most celebrated and widely recognized.

That's a result of the proliferation of sports in merchandising and on television. Today, athletes are also thrust — often unwillingly —into the limelight as role models.

Ripken has made the most of those factors. His marketability — he appears in commercials for everything from milk to grass seed — has made him fabulously wealthy. More significantly, he is a comfortable role model.

He created an adult literacy program and his professionalism helped his sport reclaim fans after a strike canceled the 1994 World Series.

A pastor once wrote *The Sun* to marvel that Ripken showed up unannounced to a child's birthday, complete with gifts, after learning that the youth was seriously ill. Said his agent, Ron Shapiro, who wrote a book about "The Power of Nice": "He is simply a nice man."

Marylanders think of themselves as humble, hard-working people. Even the state's obscure nickname, the Old Line State, refers to a feisty American Revolution regiment whose reliability impressed Gen. George Washington.

Residents of this state like to see themselves in the waterman hauling crab pots out of the bay, in the farmer toiling in the field, in the homeowner scrubbing her row house steps milky white.

Maryland also likes to see itself in Cal Ripken Jr., who approaches baseball every day as a job he badly needs — when in actuality, it is the game that needs him. •

William Donald Schaefer, renaissance man

A titan: The tempestuous boss who proved that cities could run well — even prosper

WHEN HE WAS mayor of Baltimore, his promoters insisted he was married to the city, had no other life, lived only to serve.

With William Donald Schaefer, life surpassed hype. He compiled an extraordinary record of achievement in Baltimore, devoting himself to its welfare for half a century. Machine Democrats launched him, but his own success in office gave him invincibility. Stratospheric poll ratings allowed him to leverage costly public works projects. Unseen innovations that made government more responsive were also part of his legacy.

He built momentum for a tired city with a succession of grand strokes — the National Aquarium, the Convention Center, renovation of City Hall, Harborplace, the World Trade Center, Oriole Park at Camden Yards, PSINet Stadium — a succession of Normandy-like clean-up campaigns. His political strength, his personality and the symbolism of progress enabled him to prevail against opponents who might have defeated him or his projects.

He gave his city a new Main Street — the Inner Harbor — when the old ones began to fade. He introduced a new industry — tourism — when no one thought such a thing possible in dowdy, old Baltimore.

He re-invented government a decade before that phrase was adopted by scholars and other politicians. American mayors had been ceremonial figures or defiant barons of patronage. He became a super-development chief, enlisting businessmen and neighborhood improvement leaders alike by showing why their efforts mattered.

He infused a superb staff with a measure of his derring-do. He attracted the best volunteers, young men and women who saw their personal and financial future inextricably bound up with the fate of their city.

The buffoonery of his public relations exploits — not to mention his Vesuvian temper — concealed a more discerning and instinctive leader who was willing to seem silly if it helped his city. Often criticized for being a "bricks and mortar" man, his real construction project was the spirit of Baltimoreans. He willed the city's doubting populace to give itself a break, to see its own potential.

That sort of leadership is the essence of politics. Veteran pols laughed at him a bit, thinking of him as an apolitical man, a curiosity: "Like an astronaut who didn't like to fly," one of them said.

Few of his contemporaries soared as high. A four-term member of the city council, four-term mayor and two-term governor, he came out of impatient retirement to win election as the state's comptroller — and to resume his position on the Board of Public Works where once again he could influence statewide affairs.

He made many contributions in Annapolis, visible and invisible. Against the advice of his cabinet — and against his own misgivings — he signed legislation that gave citizens and state workers access to a new system for adjudication of pension and employee grievances. Some 50,000 cases — of critical dollar-and-cents significance to individuals — are heard every year in a system thought to be a model for the nation.

In Baltimore, where his footprint is deepest, Mr. Schaefer turned the apparatus of city services into a responsive muscle. If he heard that garbage was not being picked up, he followed the trucks to find out if this was true. He appointed graffiti patrols in public housing projects, invoking a zero tolerance approach to visual pollution: he knew that every graffito or abandoned car became invisible in a day. He appointed a follow-up officer, knowing that even his most driven and conscientious staffer would succumb to procrastination.

No boss ever gave his lieutenants more room to innovate. He demanded creativity, attention to detail, respect for people — "Caring," he called it. His recruits worked fiendishly hard because they knew the rewards — and consequences — of bad concepts or poor execution.

He had his failings, to be sure. He gave far less of his energy to the schools.

He thought high-rise public housing could be saved and might not have allowed its demolition had he remained mayor. He ran roughshod over rules and regulation — and people — on occasion. He gave little help to his successor in the mayor's office. He demanded more of people than even his most loyal staffers could be expected to give. He wrote nasty letters to Marylanders who, he thought, dared to oppose him. His moods — though often useful to him — sometimes fell beneath the dignity of the office. Yet, most of these trespasses were more hurtful to him than to the city or state.

When he ran for state comptroller in 1998, voters re-endorsed his entire career. Collectively, they echoed what his loyalists said: Maryland needs his energy, his instinct for what works. At 77, when most men and women are enjoying retirement, he went back to work.

"I felt alive again," he said. Of course: For him, life is public service.

David Lewis and his bootstraps

Lawmaker: By the light of his miner's cap,
he learned Latin and law and went on to fight for workers

DAVID JOHN LEWIS' story unfolds dramatically, like a silent movie of his day:

Enter the hero, a 9-year-old miner, who picks away at Appalachian coal seams to add $10 a month in food to his family's table.

During his few work breaks, he uses the light of his cap lamp to read, thanks to the teaching of his mother and a minister at Sunday school. He begins with paperback novels, then moves on to grammar, arithmetic and science. (After a tunnel collapse, young Lewis is pulled from the dirt, his physics book still tucked into his shirt.)

His story is one thread in the changing social fabric of early 20th-century America. But his accomplishments have seldom been equaled.

His fellow miners scratched their heads at this young lad who, after his mother died when he was 12, helped raise four younger brothers and sisters while working in the mines in Allegany County — and used his late-evening hours to study. He stayed awake by holding his books with his arm crooked.

Like many poor children of his day, Lewis never attended school. The son of Welsh immigrants learned to write from Blue Back spellers.

"Little Davey," who stood all of 5 feet as an adult, shared his writing skill with other miners, composing letters for them.

He spoke regularly at Knights of Labor meetings. One evening, a newspaperman heard his reasoned arguments about improving life for workers and suggested Lewis study law.

That man "did me the greatest favor I've ever received in my life," Lewis recalled. A local attorney and priest helped him navigate through Latin and "Kent's Commentaries" on the law. Lewis still worked in the mines during those four arduous years. When he was admitted to the bar, miners proudly spread the news to colleagues as far away as West Virginia.

In 1900, the Cumberland lawyer represented leaders of a miners' strike charged with conspiracy. Though the strikers lost, Lewis became well-known in Western Maryland. In 1901, he ran for the state Senate, a Democrat winning in a heavily Republican district.

Lewis fought for mine inspections, compulsory education for children and a minimum working age of 14 for mine and factory employees. He sponsored in the General Assembly the nation's first workers' compensation law.

In 1908, he won election to the U.S. House of Representatives. He went on to serve six terms.

In Washington, he led the fight for things we take for granted today. His legislation created the parcel post, which coordinated package pickups with railway schedules to offer a less expensive way for folks in rural areas to send small packages.

He championed unemployment insurance. He was key sponsor of the Social Security Act of 1935. Franklin D. Roosevelt later hailed Lewis as "one of the American pioneers in the cause of Social Security."

Lewis was an ardent supporter of FDR's New Deal. This loyalty ultimately cost him politically.

In 1938, President Roosevelt tried to purge his enemies from Congress. He drafted Lewis, then nearly 70, to run for the U.S. Senate against conservative Democrat Millard E. Tydings. This meddling was denounced across Maryland; Lewis' image as an independent politician was compromised. Tydings easily won.

After Lewis' defeat, he served four years on the National [Railway] Mediation Board, until retiring in 1943. He returned to Cumberland, where he lived until his death in 1952 at the age of 83.

He captured his beliefs aptly when he said, "The world does not owe a man a living, but it does owe him a chance to make a living."

David Lewis knew well how precious and fleeting those chances could be. From the mines of Western Maryland to the halls of Congress, he worked to offer those opportunities to all.

Walter Sondheim sets standard for civic duty

In six decades: Charles Center, Inner Harbor, accountable schools are among his monuments

GOING STRONG, WALTER Sondheim Jr. is awaiting the millennium like everyone else. It will mark the seventh decade in which he has led efforts to improve Baltimore and Maryland public life.

When problems fester, mayors and governors put Mr. Sondheim on boards. When the problems are crucial, they make him chairman.

He is the motivator, mediator, facilitator, diplomat, tactician and consensus-builder, harnessing diverse personalities to a common goal.

Other people burn out at this sort of thing. Mr. Sondheim, 91, just gets better. Self-effacing, humorous at his own expense, he endlessly turns modesty into power and uses the power for good.

He is on no enemies list and has none. While self-important executives do not suffer fools, the endlessly courteous Walter Sondheim never met one. He also turns good manners into power. People want to please him.

Private-public partnership is where Walter Sondheim came in. Charles Center in the 1970s, the Inner Harbor in the 1980s and public school accountability in the 1990s are among his monuments. He is the consummate team player, giving fulsome credit to others.

In 1942, Mr. Sondheim was a second-generation executive of Hochschild-Kohn department store when he was drafted to head the U.S. Employment Service in Baltimore. This meant guiding workers from nonessential to essential jobs on the home front of World War II. Inspired, he joined the Navy and went to Cleveland.

There, he wangled his young family into Cleveland's public housing, which made him, a dozen years later, one of the few heads of a public housing authority with a tenant's experience.

Back home, he re-entered public service in 1948 on the city school board. In 1954, when Mayor Thomas D'Alesandro Jr. elevated Mr. Sondheim to chairman, he was also a board member of nine other civic and charitable groups.

A week later, the board was confronted by the Supreme Court decision outlawing segregated schools. The next day, Mr. Sondheim led the board in discarding race as a determining factor in school assignment. Baltimore became the first school system south of the Mason-Dixon Line to comply with that landmark ruling.

In 1957, a catch-all of city agencies was consolidated into the Baltimore Urban Renewal and Housing Administration, with Mr. Sondheim as its first chairman. He also took a back-room, cheerleading role in founding the private-sector Greater Baltimore Committee.

Downtown renewal spurred Mr. Sondheim into public service once again in the 1970s when he joined the board of Charles Center-Inner Harbor Management, then became its chairman. He had a hand in all downtown development and came to personify the Baltimore renaissance. Planners worldwide sought his advice.

Mayor Kurt L. Schmoke put Mr. Sondheim in charge of a two-year study of downtown development in 1989. Not everything recommended has come to pass, but some of its ideas live on in the Mount Vernon Cultural District and the ambitious West Side renewal plan.

William Donald Schaefer, as mayor, turned to Mr. Sondheim as a trusted adviser. When Mr. Schaefer became governor, he appointed his friend to lead a study of school performance. The result: accountability, accreditation of schools and new tests — what people nationwide laud as school reform. Maryland public education has not been the same since.

The next governor, Parris N. Glendening, talked Mr. Sondheim into joining the state school board that was implementing those reforms.

Last year, when Mr. Sondheim turned 90, school board colleagues elected him their president. This year, they did it again. He's also serving on 24 other boards and foundations.

Some thought Mr. Sondheim might slow down after the death of his beloved wife of 58 years, Janet, in 1992. In 1997, fearing he had lost competence without knowing it, he sent a request to 10 close associates, asking them to write him anonymous letters advising him when to hang up his spikes.

Their emphatic repudiations formed the basis of a *Wall Street Journal* article featuring Mr. Sondheim as poster child for elder power and vitality.

Learned texts describe the ideal public citizen, shouldering civic responsibilities, answering every call. This abstraction must look, sound and act a great deal like Walter Sondheim Jr.

Part II

Other Views
from **The Sun**

Baltimoreans I can't forget

by Rafael Alvarez

IN THIS YEAR of honoring all that is important to our century, I went fishing for local legends in the Baker-Whitely tugboat company file cabinet beneath the stained-glass windows of my Greektown row house.

I offer good-hearted goofs, thin-skinned merchants, passionate collectors, unsung angels and pains-in-the-neck; a Pikesville Rye barrel's worth of flawed and beautiful eccentrics who didn't waste a breath aiming for fame.

Soft touches like corned-beef king Seymour Attman and a sleight-of-hand sorcerer called the Great Dantini.

Bernard Livingston — the real-life uncle of Chip and Ernie Douglas of "My Three Sons" TV fame — who grew up backstage at the Clover Theater strip joint on The Block and wrote a book about it called "Papa's Burlesque House."

Lou and Judy Boulmetis, the mom-and-pop pixies who run one of the last haberdasheries in town — Hippodrome Hatters — and have resigned themselves to finding new happiness if the West Side renewal plan devours their block of Eutaw Street.

Evelyn Butterhoff, who played the piano at Rickters in Hamilton, cleaned houses for a living and declared from the stool behind her rollicking upright:

"I got a story that never ends."

Good people. People like "Miss Mary" Portera, the rabbit cacciatore-cooking "mother superior" of the St. Jude Shrine on Paca Street.

If you ran the numbers on Mrs. Portera's salary over the past half-century as chief cook and bottle washer at St. John the Baptist Roman Catholic Church, where the shrine is housed, you'd tally up a Third World paycheck. "I cooked so much the priests used to call it St. Jude's kitchen," she laughs. "All my life I did everything but hear confessions and say Mass and loved every moment of it."

The accents and hairdos and what's hidden in their shopping bags may be different, but there are spiritual siblings of Mrs. Portera in every neighborhood of the city. She explains: "You've got to give so much charity in this world."

What she shares with pilgrims seeking hope from St. Jude is matched by sharp memories of a vanished city: The Italian enclave that surrounded Lexington Market, 25-cents-an-hour piano lessons from "Miss Maggie" Winters at 314 South Poppleton Street, and the Joseph S. Hoffman tailor shop at 12 South Hanover Street, where Mrs. Portera worked as a seamstress.

The former Mary Cannatella was born at 638 Dover Street near Camden Yards. Her father, who drove a mortician's flower wagon, ran a movie house and sold fruit, grew up at 222 South Eutaw Street and played street ball with Babe Ruth.

Her grandfather ran a produce market from the front parlor of a row house at 402 South Paca Street, which was torn down for a highway. The big house the family lived in at 11 North Pearl Street was razed by the University of Maryland. The site of another home, 505 West Mulberry Street, is now a parking lot.

What Mrs. Portera lived, John Schulian tasted in the 1970s as a reporter for the *Evening Sun*.

So strong is Mr. Schulian's nostalgia for Crabtown that two decades of screen-writing success in Hollywood — where he created "Xena, Warrior Princess" — have not dimmed it. Asked to name his favorite Baltimore people, he began rattling like a windup Easter chick from Herb Rosenberg's Light Street bargain store.

"Absolutely Abe Sherman," he said, enthroning the crotchety Park Avenue newsstand owner at the head of the class. "Ellis of South Broadway who would sell you a comb for 15 cents and tell you never to come back. Dantini doing magic at the Peabody Book Store and Beer Stube. Is that place still around?"

Getting his answer, Mr. Schulian despairs: "Why do I even ask?"

After a respectful pause, he rolls on: "Polock Johnny, who was really Bohemian. Mr. Diz trying to make a living at the track by selling balloons and parking cars. Eli Hanover in the gym he ran above a bar on The Block and, of course, [burlesque queen] Blaze Starr."

In his native Los Angeles, Mr. Schulian encounters all manner of freaks, but never characters who remind him of Baltimore. "It all comes down to soul, which is absent from most of American life. It would be more fun to have Abe Sherman bitch at you than it would be to do whatever Bill Gates does for fun," he says. "Everyone I wrote about in Baltimore enjoyed life in the weird little worlds they created for themselves."

Weird little worlds inside the weird little city that struggles forward along the banks of the Patapsco.

As "Miss Bonnie" Hunt filled her bar at Fleet and Port streets with the smile of Elvis Presley, "Aunt Mary Dobkin, who ran Little League teams, taught poor kids how to bunt and chided Orioles manager Earl Weaver that the big boys didn't do enough of it. Belnord Avenue's Virginia S. Baker, the city recreation department's Queen of Fun who preached: "If it ain't decent and it ain't right, stay the hell away from it."

George Figgs, the impresario of the Orpheum Cinema who commands more minutiae about unheralded Baltimore than the Maryland Room at the Enoch Pratt Free Library. Rudolph Handel, the earnest picket who logged thousands of hours outside of *The Baltimore Sun's* Calvert Street building with a two-edged sword that said: *"Sun* Lies/*Sun* Errs."

Christopher Jensen, a plumber who often fixes pipes in exchange for artwork, lives in a house at Howard and 28th streets, which his great-grandmother bought not long after the turn of the last century, and risks his life asking motorists not to throw trash on the streets of the city he loves.

Singing Sam the Watermelon Man who bellowed "red to the rind," throughout the city's 10th Ward during the 1940s and 1950s; Paul "Hots" Watkins, an A-rabber barn boss in the days before H&S Bakery razed the Aliceanna Street stables; Louis "The Hawk" Hawkins, a barroom tap dancer who performed in gin mills from Dundalk to Pennsylvania Avenue.

John Steadman, now a *Sun* columnist, who brought horses of a different color — like the Fallsway fisherman Balls Maggio and screen painter Johnny Eck — to the larger world through his columns in the old *News American*.

Civic leader and consummate gentleman Walter Sondheim — one of the few people successful, genuine and kind enough to make anyone's list — nominates Marie Oehl von Hattersheim Bauernschmidt, a Roaring Twenties crusader for school reform.

"Because of Mrs. B," says Mr. Sondheim, "politicians stopped selling school principalships for $150 apiece out of the lobby of the Rennert Hotel."

Cops like Charlie Smoot who taught generations of rookies how to be "good police," and friendly Phil Farace, chief of the old chicken-wire lockup at Memorial Stadium.

Allan and Susan Tibbels, who traded suburban comfort to bring hope, ingenuity, elbow grease and a "New Song" to Sandtown-Winchester; Viva House's Brendan Walsh and Willa Bickham, who have given away more meals to the poor than Tio Pepe Restaurant has sold to the rich.

Veronica "Miss Fronie" Lukowski of Thames Street, who in the early 1990s was still doing her wash on a scrub board long after her grandchildren had bought her a washer and dryer.

Stan Schneider, who sells custom-cut foam out of a carnival house of bric-a-brac on Conkling Street, has lectured scores of youth about the spread of AIDS since the death of his son Jay.

Ella Thompson, who after the 1988 murder of her daughter Andrea, devoted her life to the children of West Baltimore through recreation and gardening projects. "Coach" Herman Johnson, who for 30 years has done the same at the Bentalou Recreational Center.

Talent agent Irv Klein who brought Tiny Tim to town in 1968 and his wood-scavenging, cabinet-making son, David "Blue Skies" Klein.

William D. McElroy, a Johns Hopkins biologist who paid schoolchildren a quarter for every hundred fireflies they collected for his research. And the 14-year-old boy who turned over more than 37,000 lightning bugs to Mr. McElroy in the summer of 1952.

Sowebo's dynamic, hydroponic duo of Richard Ellsberry and Gary Letteron.

"I started planting trees because it needed to be done and it felt good," says Mr. Letteron. "And then people patted me on the back for it and that felt good, too."

It feels good to do the right thing without expecting anything in return and although the old tugboat file cabinet is fat with notes on local folks who have worked toward that ideal, this list falls far short of celebrating all of them.

It is redeemed, however, with the inclusion of Amrom Taub, the peace-making rabbi of Park Heights Avenue who shuns recognition out of modesty while helping thousands of people rediscover joy in their lives.

All in Baltimore, where thanks to Abel Wolman, a pioneer in water purification, something extraordinary in our taps nurtures an endless parade of characters, with a new generation of apprentices always bringing up the rear.

Rafael Alvarez is a reporter for The Sun. *His most recent book, "Hometown Boy," is an anthology of articles published in* The Sun *over the past 20 years.*

The 101st senator

By Joseph R. L. Sterne

ON THAT GREAT day in June 1964 when the U.S. Senate at last voted to batter down the doors of discrimination in places of public accommodation, all the major civil-rights players gathered at the Capitol to celebrate. All except Clarence M. Mitchell Jr., of Baltimore, the Washington director of the NAACP.

While colleagues in the long struggle clinked glasses and paraded before the press, Mitchell made it his business to accompany Georgia Sen. Richard B. Russell Jr. on his sorrowful walk back to the Senate office building that someday would bear his name.

For two decades, Russell had led the Senate forces of the Old Confederacy in a skilled, obdurate but losing effort to maintain the segregated system that had relegated black Americans to second-class citizenship. He and Mitchell had been antagonists throughout.

They had used every parliamentary device to thwart one another. Yet here they were, a white man and a black man, both of great dignity and mutual respect, making their way almost unnoticed away from the scene of battle.

Russell was weary and disconsolate, Mitchell weary, exuberant and intent on comforting the senator. As Hubert H. Humphrey later described the scene,

Mitchell assured Russell that "he had done all he could in the struggle." Russell, in turn, said if opponents of the Civil Rights Act had not put up the fight they had, "The bill would have been unenforceable in the South."

This remarkable encounter illustrates how important personal relationships figured in the shaping of this legislation and in gaining national acceptance. Clarence Mitchell filled a pivotal role not just because he was the top lobbyist of all the civil rights groups mobilized but because he had the gravitas that commanded respect from all but the most unreconstructted racists.

For the best of reasons, he was known as "the 101st senator."

Sen. Howard Baker Jr. of Tennessee, later to become Republican majority leader, said "this magnificent lion in the lobby was a great deal more influential than most of us with seats in the chamber."

To this add Vice President Humphrey's words: "While others drew headlines and accolades, Clarence Mitchell did the day-to-day work, making every defeat, every compromise, every minor victory part of a forward movement."

President Jimmy Carter, in awarding this eminent Baltimorean the Medal of Freedom, the nation's highest civilian honor, declared that "every piece of civil rights legislation passed in the last 25 years was because of Clarence Mitchell. Without him, it could not have been done."

Growing up in modest circumstances on Stockton Street (he attended segregated P.S. No. 112 and Douglass High School before getting a degree from Lincoln University just over the Pennsylvania line), Mitchell did not encounter the full horror of racism until he had to cover a lynching on the Eastern Shore as a reporter for the *Afro-American* newspaper. That experience plus his marriage to Juanita Jackson, daughter of the matriarch of Baltimore black activism, propelled Mitchell into a lifetime of service to his race.

Thirty-nine years old when he took charge of the NAACP's Washington office, he spent much of the 1950s learning the ropes, sealing friendships with Republicans and Democrats alike and tasting the first sweet fruits of victory with the 1957 law establishing a civil rights division in the Department of Justice.

All this was but a prelude to the historic breakthroughs of the 1960s. Working incredible hours yet commuting nightly to his home in Baltimore, he found himself dealing intimately with presidents, attorneys general, members of the House and Senate, civil rights leaders and others in the corridors of power.

It was heady stuff, with victory by no means assured. More than half the Senate committee chairmanships were in the hands of Southerners. The nation was torn and distracted by war in Southeast Asia, riots over the assas-

PHOTO BY IRVING H. PHILLIPS JR., 1983

Clarence Mitchell Jr.

sination of Martin Luther King Jr. and profound political realignment.

Yet by the end of his NAACP career in 1979, Clarence Mitchell could look back on legislative accomplishments that included the public accommodations bill of 1964, the Voting Rights Act of 1965 and the 1968 law banning discrimination in housing. These were measures that transformed American society, that deserved comparison with the Emancipation Proclamation and the great amendments to the Constitution of the Civil War era.

There were many fathers to the civil rights victories; even orphans in defeat found themselves liberated. But a goodly share of the paternity belongs to Clarence Mitchell. His city honored him posthumously by naming its courthouse after him. He was, indeed, one of the leading Marylanders of the 20th century.

Joseph R. L. Sterne served as editorial page editor of The Sun *for 25 years. He also reported from London, Africa, Germany and Washington, where he covered Congress in the 1960s.*

Why they're not on my list

by Barry Rascovar

NOW THAT *The Sun's* editorial page has named its "Marylanders of the Century," debate rages over the choices. What constitutes the kind of contribution that entitles one to make the final cut?

Here's one compilation of Marylanders from the political arena who, for a variety of reasons, won't be on many "top contributor" lists.

Some were flawed figures; others had a substantial negative impact. Some served the public with valor for many years but didn't leave big enough footprints. In a few cases, time has obscured their contributions.

• **Spiro Agnew and Marvin Mandel**. The former was the only Marylander elected vice president. The latter was the best Maryland governor of the past half-century.

But their careers — and reputations — were destroyed by their shady practices.

Agnew copped a plea to avoid jail and resigned in disgrace as vice president; Mandel served jail time after two riveting trials.

Agnew was a moderate Republican governor and Baltimore county executive. He defined the ascension of suburban politicians in the 1960s. Sadly, he fathered an era of malicious name-calling in politics. His tough criticism of blacks during the 1968 Baltimore riots came to embody the GOP's blurred vision on civil rights.

Corruption charges tarnished Mr. Mandel's eight years as governor. That's a shame, because he was a political master. He skillfully gained court reforms, reorganized state government, set up a school construction program and a trust fund for mass transit and roads, and took on the National Rifle Association to pass Maryland's first gun-control law.

• **Dale Anderson and Joe Alton.** They embodied the "corruption community" that embarrassed Maryland in the 1970s. Anderson, a powerful Baltimore County executive, and Alton, an Anne Arundel County executive, were jailed for bribery. The verdict: good county managers, deaf on ethics.

And who can forget today's disgraced politician, former state Sen. Larry Young and his historic expulsion from the state Senate?

• **Alger Hiss and Whittaker Chambers.** The frightening "red scare" of the 1950s took root on a farm in Carroll County. That's where magazine editor Chambers hid documents in a pumpkin field showing that Hiss, previously a top State Department official and honored Johns Hopkins University graduate, had lied about once being in the Communist Party.

Hiss, from an old Baltimore family, was convicted of perjury. The witch hunt for communists was on.

Hiss' guilt is still hotly debated. The wild accusations that followed from Sen. Joseph McCarthy's inquiries claimed a Maryland political hero, too, when McCarthy used scurrilous smears to defeat four-term U.S. Sen. Millard E. Tydings, who dared to take on the Wisconsin senator.

• **Linda Tripp and Wallis Warfield Simpson.** Tripp laid a trap for her friend Monica Lewinsky that nearly toppled a president; Baltimore's Simpson toppled a king.

Tripp's possibly illegal tape-recorded conversations from her home in Howard County formed the basis for impeachment charges against President Clinton.

Simpson became Duchess of Windsor — after King Edward VIII of England surrendered his throne in 1936 "for the woman I love." Both women were reviled by a nation, though Wallis Simpson's love story and her royal beau's sacrifice of his crown still enthrall romanticists.

• **Jeffery and Karol Levitt.** He was convicted of stealing $14.6 million from Old Court Savings and Loan — and precipitating a terrifying run on state thrifts in 1985. Depositors lost hundreds of millions of dollars and Gov. Harry Hughes lost his chance at a U.S. Senate seat. It presaged a nationwide savings and loan debacle.

Throughout the state crisis, the Levitts' opulent lifestyle came to symbolize the egregious nature of the theft from thrift depositors.

Another villain, Tom Billman, looted his Bethesda thrift of $28 million and disappeared, skipping from country to country while living in luxury — until he was nabbed in 1992.

• **George P. Mahoney and Melvin Perkins.** Two perennial candidates, one a millionaire paving contractor, the other a Skid Row pauper.

Mahoney ran 13 times, almost always for governor or U.S. senator. He never won, but he was often a spoiler. He could be a populist or a demagogue.

He won praise as the reform-minded chairman of the racing commission in the 1940s. But in 1950, he tore the Democratic Party apart in the gubernatorial primary, leading to the defeat of Gov. William Preston Lane Jr. in November. In 1966, he helped give the nation Spiro Agnew by splintering Democratic voters with his racist rhetoric, thus handing the election for governor to Republican Agnew.

For decades, Perkins filed as a pauper candidate — for governor, mayor, even Congress. He relished his eccentricity. "We've had plenty of congressmen who went to jail," he once said. "What's wrong with a congressman who started in jail?"

He regularly brandished his discharge papers from a state mental hospital as proof of his sanity — and demanded similar evidence from his opponents.

•**William Curran and Jack Pollack.** They were two of the century's biggest bosses, controlling major chunks of Baltimore. Curran was a master manipulator, a kingmaker and attorney general in the 1940s.

Pollack was a brawler who elected governors and demanded patronage control. His release of taped conversations of Gov. J. Millard Tawes concerning Southern Maryland slot machines spurred a reform movement, which rid the state of the one-armed bandits and resulted in the eventual downfall of old-fashioned bossism.

One of Pollack's successors, William L. "Little Willie" Adams, began as a underworld numbers writer and rose to become a potent boss and patronage dispenser in black West Baltimore. He has since gained respectability as a successful Baltimore businessman.

• **Marie Oehl von Hattersheim Bauernschmidt and Hyman Pressman.** She terrorized politicians in the 1920s, 1930s and 1940s; he did the same in the 1950s and into the 1960s until he was elected city comptroller in 1963. He then served 28 years as the city's self-proclaimed fiscal watchdog.

"Mrs. B" crusaded for better schools, denounced politicians on radio and campaigned for social causes at community meetings. She harangued Mayor

Howard L. Jackson for being a drunk — a factor in his decision not to run for re-election. She was a one-person investigative team.

Pressman saw himself as "champion of the little guy."

He fought City Hall for decades, through court suits and publicity stunts. In office he proved a tightwad intent on exposing waste.

His fame came, though, from his love of marching in parades, dancing at any hint of music and reading his pedestrian poetry.

• **Louis L. Goldstein and J. Millard Tawes.** Between the two, they served 100-plus years in state offices, including a stunning 64 years as comptroller (four terms for Tawes, 10 for Goldstein). Tawes rose higher, as a two-term governor, then returning as Maryland's first natural resources secretary and as state treasurer.

They were workhorses, though Goldstein turned his corny, relentless campaigning and his slogan, "God bless you all real good," into unbeatable political gimmicks.

Street priest

by Dan Rodricks

HIS ATTEMPT TO save the world, one man at a time, always kept Chuck Canterna on the run and breathless.

The first time I met him, on a sidewalk in Little Italy, he was too busy — and too modest, anyway — to talk about his work. For most of the day, a heroin addict had been going through withdrawal in a second-floor room on Fawn Street, and now he was headed into a night of cold-turkey turmoil. Chuck planned to spend the weekend with him. We heard a hideous moan from the window of the junkie's bedroom, and Chuck dashed across the street and disappeared into the house.

The next time, Chuck was dressed in a dark windbreaker, kneeling on a sidewalk orange from neon light near The Block, trying to stir awake a sleeping man. The man was Curtis Sigler, a homeless, frost-bitten alcoholic who lived in vacant houses when he was sober and rational enough to come in from the cold.

Chuck Canterna visited him every day, made sure he had food, helped him find faith and instilled in him a spirit for change. It worked for a while, too. Sigler became a new man in the early 1980s. He stopped drinking, pulled himself out of the gutter, shed the tattered overcoat and donned a new suit. But the happy ending ended one fine day, and Sigler vanished into a whiskey mist. Still, Chuck Canterna went out to find him again, to try and save him again.

Father Chuck, I should say. He's a Catholic priest. People used to call him the Street Priest. He was charismatic and athletic, always in a mad dash, on foot or bicycle, to save the world — one man, one woman, one child at a time. His hair was dark and his eyes were full of light. His spirit was always high.

He got the call in the 1960s, at a time when many priests were starting to leave the church. Canterna wanted something special; he decided during seminary days that his priesthood would be based in the street. He wanted to work with the poor and needy of an American city.

A bishop in the diocese of Pittsburgh, Chuck's hometown, had other ideas. He wanted to assign Chuck to a suburban parish. "I have enough radical, inner-city priests," the bishop said. Chuck was denied ordination. He went to work in a steel mill for a while, but remained committed to the call. He was eventually ordained and wound up in Maryland, with the ministry he wanted.

By the time I met him, he had a room at St. Vincent's Church, on Front Street, near the main post office in Baltimore. But Chuck was hardly ever in the rectory and difficult to contact. He was on the street at all hours of day and night.

Someone in St. Vincent's parish gave him a new winter coat; Chuck gave it to a homeless man. Someone would bake him a casserole; Chuck would give it away.

One day, my fiance and I managed to get him alone for a few minutes, to discuss our wedding plans. There was a knock on the door — a homeless, unemployed man with three children had come to Front Street looking for help. Chuck fetched two bags of groceries, excused himself, then dashed off to help the man find lodging for his family.

(Amazingly, we got this priest to a church in Pennsylvania, three hours from Baltimore, just in time to marry us the following September.)

Of all people who endure the hard sweat of trying to repair the broken men, women and children among us — social workers, addictions counselors, volunteers at soup kitchens and shelters, doctors, nurses, paramedics and psychiatrists — Chuck's commitment never ceased. He never burned out. He never gave up.

Through the last 20 years of this century, he's remained committed to bringing faith and hope to the desperate, the destitute, the diseased and the doomed.

He's been a chaplain in the Baltimore City Correctional Center and the Maryland Penitentiary since the early 1980s.

He's worked with the most violent men in our midst. He's counseled drug addicts, men with AIDS, and three murderers who were executed by the state in the 1990s. He's been a mediator, a listener, a preacher, a healer.

His priesthood went inside shortly after the assassination of Archbishop Romero in El Salvador in 1980. "That made me want to work to make the world a less violent place," he said from the "Super Max" prison one night, when I managed to get Chuck on the phone. We hadn't spoken in years. His voice was still strong, a little breathless. He was still passionate about his work.

"God is good and the light is bright," he said.

And this from a man who, every day for the last two decades, has been in close contact with killers and rapists. It would seem to most people an immensely daunting task — trying to bring hope and faith to men who had been sentenced to life in prison.

"I plant the seeds, God does the watering," Chuck says. "I

PHOTO BY CLARENCE B. GARRETT, 1978

Rev. Charles Canterna

love the work. When you serve others, the blessings come back to you."

The men in the penitentiary are angry, mean, aloof. Some are hard-nosed atheists. "The first three I approach might reject me," Chuck says.

"And then the fourth, the fifth, the sixth, the seventh, the eighth, the ninth. But then the 10th — that guy might be open to God, open to the spirit. He might respond. I might be able to get him to go inside himself and find meaning and purpose to his life, and maybe a light comes on and the guy finds the spirit. I'm just there to help him connect to the spirit."

And that's how the world is saved — one man at a time.

Dan Rodricks has written a local column for the Evening Sun *and* The Sun *since 1979. His collection of columns, "Mencken Doesn't Live Here Anymore," was published in 1989.*

Running the B&O in tough times

by Frederick N. Rasmussen

HOWARD EDWARD SIMPSON, who rose from an office boy to president of the Baltimore & Ohio Railroad and later was a co-architect of the C&O/B&O affiliation in 1961, was one of the nation's most highly respected and prominent railroaders.

In a colorful and varied career that spanned nearly 75 years, Simpson held 25 jobs by the time he was named B&O president in 1953, and took control of the venerable railroad. He oversaw its operations from a third-floor corner office in B&O's landmark headquarters building at Baltimore and Charles streets.

His years as president were troublesome. The rail industry faced growing competition from airplanes, trucks, automobiles, buses and inland waterway traffic.

By 1958, with the country locked in a recession and coal and steel carloadings declining followed by a disastrous 116-day steel strike, Simpson was forced to make economies, cutting employees by nearly 50 percent. Merger talks were in the air.

Automobiles were depriving the B&O of passenger revenues on its historic Royal Blue Route between Washington and New York. Simpson made the momentous decision to withdraw the passenger service.

"He came into the B&O at an extremely bad time," said Herbert H. Harwood, a rail historian.

Harwood described Simpson as being "very unusual in the railroad business because railroad presidents didn't come out of the passenger department in the old days."

Simpson inherited an organization that dated to the time of Daniel Willard, the legendary B&O president who ran the railroad for over 30 years.

"What Simpson needed was new blood and new ideas," said Harwood.

Fearing that a New York Central and Pennsylvania Railroad merger would destroy B&O markets, Simpson proposed in 1958 to his counterpart on the Chesapeake & Ohio Railway, Walter J. Tuohy, an affiliation: The B&O had such resources as coal, timber and industry; the C&O had cash and credit but little traffic.

Thus the idea, born in the back seat of a Washington taxi that the two railroad executives were sharing, later blossomed into the Chessie System and today's mega-railroad, CSX.

"He was an effective salesman and that was his main talent," said Harwood of the man who was the last "pure" president of the railroad founded in Baltimore in 1827 as America's first common-carrier railroad.

Simpson's tenure also saw a complete conversion to diesel engines. And he was responsible for establishing the B&O Railroad Museum in Baltimore in 1953.

"He always felt that anything that was favorable to Baltimore was favorable to the B&O," said James D. Dilts, who interviewed Simpson while researching his book on the B&O.

"The B&O kept its traffic longer than most and he devoted his efforts to keeping its passenger traffic," Dilts said. Simpson saved the B&O.

"Simpson was slightly ahead of the big merger wave of the 1960s, and in fact, the B&O remained independent until 1987 and managed to outlive such rail giants as the Pennsylvania and New York Central railroads."

Born in 1896 in Jersey City, N.J., the son of a traveling salesman, Simpson spent his youth watching trains steam in and out of the yards that surrounded that city. As a youngster, he sprawled on the floor memorizing railroad timetables his father had brought from his trips to amuse his young son.

After the death of his parents and with siblings to help support, Simpson dropped out of school and joined the Central Railroad of New Jersey as a $20-a-month office boy in the passenger department.

Realizing by the mid-1920s that private autos and buses were cutting into the Central's revenues on its Atlantic City service, Simpson introduced the

PHOTO BY ROBERT F. KNIESCHE, 1953

Howard E. Simpson

reserved coach seat. This idea proved so successful that by World War II it had become an industry standard.

His career blossomed in 1931 when he joined the B&O as Eastern passenger agent in New York. He rose like a rocket through the B&O hierarchy.

Simpson spent the final years of his life still going to his 22nd-floor Charles Center office where he served in the role of procounsul for the Chessie System and made his vast knowledge and experience available to younger railroaders.

He continued to testify on railroad matters before congressional committees as well as on rate cases before the Interstate Commerce Commission.

"His grasp of the problems reached beyond the myriad of schedules, routes and services... He wrestled diligently to resurrect the B&O, while also giving unselfishly of himself to other corporate and cultural institutions. His death closes a chapter in railroad history," said a 1985 editorial in *The Sun*.

Frederick N. Rasmussen has been a member of The Sun *staff since 1973.*

Ten who impacted the state and nation

by Gregory Kane

PERSONS OF THE century — much like *Time* magazine's "Man of the Year" and "Woman of the Year" — should logically be selected on the basis of the impact they've had on a state and national scale.

Ten come almost immediately to mind, so a top ten list is perhaps in order. Unlike David Letterman, I'll go in descending order.

1. H. L. Mencken. The "Sage of Baltimore" gets the No. 1 slot not only for his bristling commentaries and pointed jibes at the rich, powerful and hypocritical. Much has been written about Mencken's impact on both Baltimore and American arts and letters. But his impact goes much deeper.

Richard Wright, the African-American author of the 1940 novel "Native Son," credited Mencken with being the inspiration for his writing career. It was while in the South that Wright overheard several white men talking about Mencken in expressions of outrage. Wright managed to finagle some of Mencken's books from the local whites-only library and took a peak for himself. It was from reading Mencken that Wright realized words could be weapons.

Wright went on to influence black novelists Ralph Ellison and James Baldwin, who in turn influenced an entire generation of black writers behind them. When you consider that one critic said the publication of "Native Son" changed American culture forever, it puts the enormity of Mencken's influence in its proper perspective.

2. Clarence M. Mitchell Jr. If he were just the father of former state Sen. Clarence Mitchell III and City Councilman Michael Mitchell; grandfather of state Sen. Clarence Mitchell IV and City Councilman Keiffer Mitchell Jr. that would be accomplishment enough. But Mitchell Jr. is actually responsible for getting the civil rights legislation sought by activists like Martin Luther King Jr. and James Farmer passed. His lobbying efforts in that endeavor led to his nickname, the "101st senator."

3. Thurgood Marshall. He actually had more impact as an NAACP Legal Defense and Education Fund lawyer than as the first black Supreme Court justice. Marshall argued and won many landmark cases that ended legal segregation, including 1954's Brown vs. Board of Education before the U.S. Supreme Court.

4. Thomas J. D'Alesandro Jr. As a three-term mayor of Baltimore, he was responsible for the city's first renaissance and brought the Orioles and Colts to town.

5. Lillie Carroll Jackson. She revitalized Baltimore's NAACP branch and was the mother of Juanita Jackson Mitchell, wife of Clarence Mitchell Jr. Her activism paved the way for desegregation in Baltimore. My mother's favorite Jackson story is how she would go into downtown desegregated department stores and raised hell when she was refused service. Nervous managers, realizing who she was, simply told store clerks "For God's sakes, wait on her!"

6. Juanita Jackson Mitchell. She was the first black woman to practice law in Maryland. While husband Clarence was lobbying senators in Washington, Juanita was fighting segregation and racism in Baltimore. Extra kudos should go to Jackson-Mitchell for hauling the Baltimore Police Department into court in the mid-1960s to stop them from searching without warrants the homes of black citizens in the wake of two cop killings.

7. Abel Wolman. If you've heard Baltimore's drinking water tastes better than many other cities in the country, you have Wolman to thank.

8. Kweisi Mfume. He rose from the mean streets of Baltimore to be a city councilman and a U.S. congressman. He revitalized the NAACP and brought it back from the brink of disaster. And he did all this before the age of 50.

9. Spiro Agnew. Yes, he had to resign as vice president because of a kickback scandal that happened when he was Baltimore County executive. Yes, as governor of Maryland he idiotically and cynically blamed Baltimore's black leaders for the riots that occurred in the wake of Martin Luther King Jr.'s assassination in 1968. But as Vice President Agnew, he was the conservative Republican pit bull who took the verbal war to liberal Democrats, put the poor wusses on the defensive and paved the way for a Ronald Reagan presidency and the eventual Republican takeover of Congress in 1994. He had more national impact than he's usually given credit for.

10. Barry Levinson. No Marylander this century has had more influence on the art of film.

Gregory Kane is a native Baltimorean and Sun *columnist who started as a free-lance Opinion-Commentary writer in 1984.*

The gift of literacy

by Sara Engram

LONGEVITY IS A useful ally in research. When Margaret Byrd Rawson set out to document the progress of 56 school boys, 20 of them identified as dyslexic, she was a young mother caught up in the absorbing project of establishing a small private school near Philadelphia.

By the time she sat down to compile her results for publication in the 1960s, her subjects were in mid-career and she was retiring from the faculty of Hood College in Frederick. A quarter-century later, as she was entering her 90s, she appended four new chapters and re-published her landmark book as "Dyslexia Over the Lifespan: A Fifty-Five Year Longitudinal Study."

By then, "Rawson's boys" were reaching conventional retirement ages. Their careers provided ample proof that, given appropriate instruction, dyslexics are as capable of high levels of success as non-dyslexics. Among her subjects, the dyslexics were more likely than their non-dyslexic peers to excel, with more than half of them earning graduate degrees.

Rawson's research drew on keen observations, a lively intelligence and the imagination to see opportunities where most people saw problems. Where others dwelled on theories of how children learn to read and why

PHOTO BY KIM HAIRSTON, 1998

Margaret Rawson

some otherwise capable youngsters can't seem to master the skill, she rolled up her sleeves and showed what it took for them to break the code of written language.

She first encountered dyslexia in a boy at the School at Rose Valley, the progressive school where Rawson and other educators were committed to educating "the whole child," rather than simply teaching skills. Despite the supportive atmosphere, a sixth-grader named Peter just couldn't seem to learn to read.

Rawson, then serving as the school's librarian, took up the challenge of helping Peter. Eventually, she found a neurologist in New York, Dr. Samuel T. Orton, who in conjunction with a psychologist and educator, Anna Gillingham, had devised a way to help children like Peter gain mastery of sounds, letters, words and sentences.

She seized on the Orton-Gillingham method, a multi-sensory approach to teaching the sounds and letters of English that is now recognized as the key to turning dyslexics into competent readers. It worked for Peter — he later earned a Ph.D. in chemistry from Harvard — and it set Margaret Rawson on a life's mission.

To spread the word, Rawson helped establish the Orton Dyslexia Society, now the International Dyslexia Association. Her research and her ability to converse as easily with neurologists about brain research as with a teacher dealing with a particularly challenging pupil made her an effective intellectual voice for the organization.

Her work with children like Peter convinced her that in traditional school settings, dyslexia, with its tendency to scramble or reverse sounds or letters, may be a "disability," but that in fact dyslexia usually brings strong aptitudes in other areas, such as conceptual or visual abilities. She aimed to show that labeling it simply a "disability" — rather than a form of intellectual diversity — reveals more about the limitations of traditional schooling than about the aptitudes of dyslexic youngsters.

Acting on that conviction, Rawson has helped to set up more than a half-dozen schools. One of the first was the Jemicy School in Baltimore County, which opened in 1973 with the mission of educating bright dyslexic children. Her ties with the school remain strong. As her 100th birthday approached in the summer of 1999, she made the familiar trip from her farmhouse near Frederick — the area where she has resided for over half a century — to the Jemicy campus. More than 300 people gathered to celebrate and show their affection for the "grande dame of dyslexia."

Few people have lived a century as energetically, as effectively or as joyfully as Margaret Byrd Rawson. And few educators have earned more heartfelt gratitude from generations of students and their families. Her trailblazing work in effective education for dyslexics has given them the priceless gift of literacy — and the opportunity for a lifetime of achievement.

Sara Engram, an assistant metropolitan editor, was for many years a deputy editorial page editor for The Sun *and the* Evening Sun.

Home deliveries

by Hal Piper

FOR A FEW years after World War II, retail commerce still came to our residential neighborhood. The fish man, the vegetable man and the milkman made regular rounds. A knife-sharpening man and door-to-door salesmen like the Fuller brush man showed up irregularly, but often enough that we knew their names.

There was even a paper boy who delivered the *Evening Sun*. He was in my Cub Scout den and lived down the street. I aspired to be a paper boy, too, but my father thought kids should play or study, not work.

We had the occasional "A-rab" with colorful horse-drawn wagon, but we lived too far out in the suburbs to see many of these. Our tradesmen drove trucks or vans that carried their wares and equipment.

Mr. Ermer was the fish man. I didn't like fish, but I liked Mr. Ermer, a slight, snaggle-toothed, curly-haired man. He had a panel truck with back doors that opened out and revealed a built-in fish shop complete with scaling board, hanging balance scale and, of course, a tub of shaved ice with whole fish — eyes and all — in it. The truck smelled fishy, but not too fishy.

After my mother had made her choice — rock, shad, perch, flounder — Mr.

Ermer pulled the fish out of the shaved ice, beheaded it, scaled it, wrapped it and weighed it. It's just what they do behind the supermarket counter today, but it was much more interesting observed up close at your front curb.

The vegetable man came late, sometimes after dark. He spoke in a nasal wheeze and tucked his pencil behind his ear to get it out of the way, and I liked him, too. He taught me the word "rutabaga" and gave me an order pad. I wrote imaginary orders on it for weeks.

For a summer or two, the ice man brought cooling from his depot on Susquehanna Avenue in Towson, next to the Ma and Pa railroad station. You would buy a 20-to-50-pound block of ice, which the ice man chipped and shaved out of a much larger block. Then he carried it with tongs into the kitchen and fitted it into the upper shelf of your ice box.

I can remember when we got our first electric refrigerator, and I guess everyone else must have got one about the same time, because one summer the ice man no longer made deliveries.

The others stopped coming, too. By the time I was in junior high school, only the ice-cream truck still visited our neighborhood.

Mr. Dawson was our mailman. He had a mustache like my dad's and I liked him, too. He was one of the few Negroes (as they were called then) that we would see regularly in our neighborhood. A few years later he had some prominence in local civil-rights demonstrations and we were proud of him.

The other Negro I knew was Miss Martha, the cleaning lady. She showed me pictures of her little boy, who was a couple of years younger than I.

I liked Miss Martha, too, but we disagreed about one thing. When Joe Louis defended his heavyweight boxing championship against Jersey Joe Walcott she was for Louis. I liked Jersey Joe — cool name! Seizing the teachable moment, my dad explained to me the symbolic importance of Joe Louis for Negroes. My dad was for Joe Louis. So I transferred by allegiance, and Miss Martha and I were reconciled. And Joe Louis won — hooray!

Miss Martha, Mr. Dawson, the ice man, the vegetable man, Mr. Ermer — can they be Marylanders of the Century? Certainly. The tradespeople and service workers who came into your neighborhood gave life texture and widened the horizons of mid-century children.

In a 34-year career at The Sun, *Hal Piper has been a foreign correspondent and Opinion-Commentary page editor. He now edits* Sun Journal.

Conscience of Baltimore

by Joan Jacobson

FOR NEARLY A third of the century, Willa Bickham and Brendan Walsh have been the conscience of Baltimore.

Viva House, their Catholic Worker House of Hospitality and Resistance in Southwest Baltimore, has responded to the needs of the city's poor since it opened in October 1968, always warning that the city renaissance would only make life worse for the underclass.

Back then, the young married couple had no idea they would become a permanent oasis for the increasingly desperate population of unemployed, hungry families, eventually feeding 270 people a day, three days a week.

When they began, their row house at 26 South Mount Street was a haven for protesters of the Vietnam war, specifically those members of the Catonsville Nine awaiting trial for burning draft board records. Later it became home to other war resisters, then to single alcoholic men, and later a shelter for women and children.

But in the middle 1980s, when homelessness, hunger and drug use increased as the federal government cut housing funds to the poor, Viva House once again changed with the times and became a soup kitchen. Today,

Walsh and Bickham will tell you that the name "soup kitchen" is no longer applicable. Children, says Bickham, who is a nurse, don't like soup, so Viva House serves other nutritious foods to the many families who come to them now. They even cleverly hide spinach in the lasagna.

What sets Walsh and Bickham apart from other do-gooders and organizations that help the needy — in addition to their longevity — is that they have established their own system of volunteers and donors of food, without any help from government or the Catholic Church.

This enables them to pursue their public protests of City Hall policies they believe hurt the poor.

Other groups butting heads with a powerful mayor found their funds cut off in the 1970s and 1980s. Eventually, leaders of these city-financed groups learned to keep their opinions to themselves. But not Walsh and Bickham. Their unorthodox positions — whether trumpeted by Walsh in a one-man protest outside City Hall or in newspaper stories — have often shocked even the liberal establishment.

Opposing historic preservation, development of the Inner Harborr, or demolition of the dangerous public housing high-rise buildings was seen by many as heresy. They called uprooting the poor a new form of "ethnic cleansing" and pointed out that Americans no longer have a right to a home and a job. They came to believe that their country was waging a war on the lower class.

The couple has steadfastly maintained the "Baltimore renaissance" did little to help the poor. If you judge by the growing stream of hungry people who come through their colorful flower garden several times a week, they are right.

PHOTO BY JOSEPH DIPAOLA JR., 1971

Willa Bickham

When nearby Union Square — with its H. L. Mencken House — became a historic district, Walsh and Bickham warned it would increase property taxes in the neighborhood and push out the poor. When Harborplace was built, using millions of dollars in federal neighborhood-development funds for brick sidewalks and bulkheads, they argued the new harbor glitz would never trickle down to the poor.

When the notorious Murphy Homes public housing project

was imploded, they were there to protest. Where did the people go who lived there? Were they given subsidized housing, they asked skeptically? Why weren't the houses built in their place affordable to the poor?

Instead, they know the families they feed in their clean, cheerful dining rooms, live in overcrowded slums — three families to an apartment. And now there's a new term — "working poor" — to describe the people with jobs created at Inner Harbor hotels because these jobs don't pay as well as the thousands of manufacturing jobs lost over the last half of this century.

PHOTO BY IRVING PHILLIPS JR., 1975

Brendan Walsh

As the 20th century closes and Walsh and Bickham grow into their late 50s, their solid organization of volunteers continues. Catholic and Jewish friends, retired city workers, students from a posh private school, fellow pacifists and champions of an independent Ireland all come to serve and cook food at Viva House.

Now a new generation is continuing Walsh and Bickham's work.

Their daughter, Kate Walsh-Little, a teacher who grew up with her parents in an apartment above Viva House, runs a summer camp and tutoring program for neighborhood children. Her lawyer-husband, David Walsh-Little, offers free legal counsel to the poor from his Sowebo Center for Justice next door. By the time the next century begins, they hope to expand into another row house up the block and raise their baby daughter there.

Although Walsh and Bickham never expected hunger and homelessness to become such a fixture in Baltimore, they have kept Viva House open out of a sad necessity. They'll be there working with the poor, as long as they are needed.

Joan Jacobson, a reporter for the Evening Sun *and* The Sun *for 25 years, has covered neighborhoods, housing, poverty, politics and investigative stories on the misuse of public funds. She was also the* Evening Sun's *dance critic.*

Maryland's 20th-century art scene

by John Dorsey

IN THE VISUAL arts, Maryland in the 20th century saw enormous institutional and collecting developments, and much individual creative vitality.

By 1900, we already had the Maryland Institute, Maryland Historical Society and Peabody Institute (which then collected art), but Henry Walters had just begun the vast enlargement of his father's collection, and the Cone sisters got going in 1901. The Baltimore Museum of Art came along in 1914 and got its own home in 1929.

Herewith a baker's dozen plus one of those who have contributed significantly to the 20th-century art scene.

Henry Walters (1848-1931) inherited his father William's collection of French academic and Asian art in 1894, and built upon it a monumental collection, especially of Western art from ancient Egypt down to impressionist paintings. He housed it in a renaissance palace and left everything to the city and the people of Baltimore.

Sisters **Claribel Cone** (1864-1929) and **Etta Cone** (1870-1949) amassed one of the largest Matisse collections in the world (500 works) and art by many other great modern artists including Cezanne, Gauguin, van Gogh and

Picasso. Etta left it all to the Baltimore Museum of Art, plus $400,000 to build a wing for it.

Adelyn Breeskin (1896-1986) in 32 years as curator and director of the Baltimore Museum of Art attracted the Garrett Collection of old master art, the Lucas Collection of 19th-century art (together about 40,000 works, mostly prints) and the Cone Collection of modern art: an incomparable feat.

A. Aubrey Bodine (1906-1970) in a half-century as a *Sun* and salon photographer, won international recognition and countless prizes. His love was Maryland's landscape and seascape; he worked primarily in the romantic pictorialist tradition, but was conscious of modernism and produced near-abstract pictures as well.

Herman Maril (1908-1986) won universal admiration and affection as both painter and teacher. His landscapes and interiors approach the threshold of abstraction without ever crossing it; his love of light, color, nature and his fellow creatures endows his work with quiet joy.

Reuben Kramer (1909-1999) had a career as a sculptor that spanned seven decades, from the 1920s to the 1990s. He executed some portrait sculpture, notably of Thurgood Marshall, but he specialized in small-scale bronzes of the female figure which have been compared with chamber music in their intimacy and charm.

Keith Martin (1911-1983) produced most of his mature work after he settled in Baltimore in the late 1940s. His paintings, drawings and collages occupy a territory between surrealism and abstraction, and combine mysteriously elusive imagery with deep lyric beauty.

Eugene Leake (born 1911) came to Baltimore in 1961 as president of the Maryland Institute, College of Art and spent 13 years transforming it from a mediocrity to a nationally respected college. Then he retired and over the last quarter of a century has achieved wide recognition as a landscape painter whose work possesses a rare combination of profundity and optimism.

Morris Louis (1912-1962) was born in Baltimore and educated at the Maryland Institute, College of Art, but pursued his career in Washington. He was one of those who, following the abstract expressionists, developed an art in which color dominated. His canvases, stained with broad washes of color, possess a fluid serenity.

Grace Hartigan (born 1922) moved to Baltimore in 1960 after coming to the fore as a "second generation" New York abstract expressionist in the 1950s. Over the last four decades she has persisted in producing an art whose constant vitality reflects an ever-renewing vision; as a teacher, she brings out qualities young artists didn't even know they had.

Raoul Middleman (born 1935) through his expressive brush stroke reveals his restless, inquiring mind and enormous energy, and fills his paintings with intensity. He is best known for landscape, but his densely populated allegories are among his best works, and his portraits reveal more about his subjects than they may want to acknowledge.

Tom Miller (born 1945) was in his 40s before he began transforming old furniture into boldly colorful, gently humorous satires on racial stereotypes which have earned him a horde of collectors and admirers. Nobody doesn't like Tom Miller's art.

Joyce Scott (born 1948) comes from an artistic family and was educated in Maryland and Mexico. She draws on multiple influences including her African-American background to create everything from bead sculptures to multi-media prints to installations and performance art. Her works deal with social issues such as race, gender and crime, and possess wit and bite, but also compassion for those who need it most.

It should be noted that all 10 of the artists above had or have some connection with the Maryland Institute, a testament to its prodigious contributions to the art of Baltimore and Maryland.

John Dorsey worked for The Sun *for 36 years as a features writer on the arts, book-review editor, restaurant reviewer and art critic.*

Eradicating a terrible disease

by Jonathan Bor

WHAT DISEASE HAS inflicted the greatest toll on the human race?

A few hints: It spent 10,000 years on earth, succumbing in 1977 to a global eradication campaign. Its marks can be found on Egyptian mummies. In the 16th century, it was the killer blow dealt by Spaniards to the great civilizations of Mexico and Peru. In 1706, it wiped out one-third of Iceland's population.

In the 20th century, it killed an estimated 300 million people, more than the combined carnage of all wars fought through World War II.

The killer disease? Smallpox.

It is no exaggeration to say that the man who led its conquest is one of the great heroes of 20th-century medicine.

Dr. Donald Anslie Henderson, a graduate of the Johns Hopkins School of Public Health and its future dean, initially refused when the World Health Organization asked him in 1966 to lead its campaign to eliminate smallpox. It wasn't just the logistics of reaching millions of people in remote corners of the world that worried him. It was the politics: gaining the cooperation of foreign leaders, and bringing a common purpose to the WHO itself, which suffered from political divisions.

D.A. Henderson signed on because his employer, the U.S. Public Health Service, ordered him to. He thought he could set up the program and leave, perhaps after 18 months.

He stayed for a decade.

Henderson, a tall, dignified man with swept-over hair that hinted of Will Rogers, honed his organizational skills while director of the surveillance section of the U.S. Centers for Disease Control. This was the division that tracked outbreaks of diseases like measles, hepatitis and influenza; leading it meant working with local governments and organizing disease-trackers across the country into a detective force.

On the world stage, he proved a master. Under his leadership, the WHO organized thousands of local physicians, nurses and lay health workers in countries of Latin America, Africa and Asia. They would deliver 250 million vaccine doses per year over the course of the 11-year campaign, trudging through swamps of Bangladesh, across deserts in Ethiopia and through crowded slums of India.

The campaign scored its first major victories in Brazil, Indonesia and Africa, then faced its toughest battles in South Asia, where the disease was most prevalent. Along the way, there were disasters and near-disasters. In Bangladesh, for instance, the disease seemed under control when civil war drove thousands of people to refugee camps in India — and into the heart of a smallpox epidemic. Many caught the disease, then brought it home when independence was declared.

In India, the task was grueling, not just because of the huge population — three-quarters of a billion people by the 1970s — but also by a national rail system that kept people constantly in motion.

Henderson succeeded, in part, because he maintained a research program that produced ingenious solutions to problems that might have proved fatal.

Smallpox is a highly contagious disease caused by a virus that travels through the air, killing a third of the people it infects.

Despite its virulence, scientists realized they didn't have to vaccinate whole populations, a task that would have been impossible. Instead, they adopted a practical strategy of encirclement: locating and isolating sick patients, then vaccinating everyone in the immediate area.

The vaccine breaks down in the heat, so they freeze-dried it. When they realized their vaccine supply would never last, they invented a two-pronged needle that holds just the right amount without wasting a drop. This made their inventory last five times as long.

In 1967, the disease afflicted 10 million people around the world. By 1975, a girl from an impoverished family in Bangladesh became the last case of severe smallpox. Two years later, an Ethiopian man became the last person to have the mild form.

Dr. Myron Levine, a vaccine researcher who organized the campaign in a populous district of Bangladesh, flew into the country with Henderson in the tense moments after the country's president was assassinated.

"He knew everything that was going on in every country," said Levine, who now heads vaccine research at the University of Maryland Medical Center. "He knew all the people and was extremely supportive of them. He was a true leader."

PHOTO BY PAUL HUTCHINS, 1977

Dr. D. A. Henderson

In the center of the discussion, Henderson would encourage the workers, telling them how they fit into the total picture of eradication. At times like these, Henderson's habit of moving people from one country to the next proved useful. Workers who had spent time in Ethiopia would explain what it was like to travel across the desert in blistering heat.

"They'd say, 'Quit complaining. It's a piece of cake'," Levine recalled.

Noted Henderson: "This has to be the greatest victory over any disease. We've never eradicated any other disease, and people who contributed to this were just incredible." Though it is hard to quantify the accomplishment, experts say the campaign has saved some 50 million lives since victory was declared.

Henderson, who lives in Guilford with his wife, Nana, served as dean of the Johns Hopkins School of Public Health from 1977 through 1990. Today, he heads a Hopkins institute that works to raise consciousness about another looming threat — that of bioterrorism.

Jonathan Bor has covered medicine and public health for The Sun *since 1988. He is a native of Washington, D.C., and previously worked for the Syracuse (N.Y.)* Post-Standard.

They never said it would be easy

by Michael Olesker

THURGOOD MARSHALL AND Clarence Mitchell Jr. were the spiritual godfathers of my generation of American school children, the first to look across our classrooms and see skin color different than our own.

These two men helped give a conscience to an America that gave lip service to great ideals about brotherhood but resolutely refused to embrace some of them until halfway through the 20th century.

In the third grade at Sir Robert Eden Elementary School No. 20, near North Avenue and Harford Road in East Baltimore, not one of us in Mrs. Poole's class, not one white child in a room filled with white children, in an entire public school filled with white children, imagined the world being invented in that spring of 1954.

In the civil rights revolution of mid-century America, Martin Luther King Jr. would win the grandest headlines, but it was these two men from West Baltimore, Marshall in the federal courtrooms and Mitchell working the back rooms of Capitol Hill, who changed not only the lives of children, but the legal rights of adults when they went looking for a job, or a decent house, or the right to cast a vote.

That spring of 1954, the time of Brown vs. Board of Education, that time when the man in the White House, Dwight D. Eisenhower, cringed from discussion of race, that spring when black people couldn't drink at certain water fountains in the South, couldn't sit in certain bus seats or use restrooms along certain highways, couldn't buy a meal in certain Baltimore restaurants or swim in certain public pools or ride the roller coaster at a place called Gwynn Oak Park, everything that had separated children by skin color in the public schools such as P.S. No. 20 in East Baltimore was about to begin changing.

In that time, there was Thurgood Marshall, in the midst of his 25-year career as counsel for the National Association for the Advancement of Colored People, winning 29 of 32 cases he argued before the U.S. Supreme Court, including the 1954 Brown vs. Board of Education decision that tore down the historic law on segregated school systems.

And there was Clarence Mitchell Jr., the NAACP's chief lobbyist, the director of its Washington office, the patriarch of the black family most prominent in Baltimore politics, whose work helped end the nation's legal and "traditional" practices of racial segregation.

The efforts of Marshall and Mitchell touched all who live in America, and ultimately made us a better people.

They never said integration would be easy.

They only said it was fair.

Which is why it's worth mentioning that spring of 1954, and the Brown decision outlawing school segregation, and the places such as Mrs. Poole's third grade class at P.S. No. 20.

It is only one illustration, but surely it mirrors others. In those days, my family lived in the Latrobe Homes, a government-subsidized housing project. We had a man who later ran for mayor of Baltimore who came out of those projects, named Carl Stokes, who arrived two years after my family moved away.

In my time, there were government projects for white people, and separate projects for black people. My family lived there because my father, having dropped out of college for World War II, brought us to Baltimore while he went back to school. When he graduated and found work, we moved to middle class suburbia.

Carl Stokes' family moved in when certain parts of American life were beginning to integrate — housing projects, but not necessarily job opportunities. My family lived in the projects for four years; Stokes' family stayed for 13.

When I left the white projects every morning, I walked north along Aisquith Street, past row houses where all the residents were black, on my way to the public school that was all white.

When Stokes arrived a few years later, his father, a product of the city's segregated schools, was grateful to find an assembly-line job on Hanover Street. What money he had, he used to put his son into a little Catholic school on Central Avenue, until Carl won an academic scholarship years later to Loyola High.

It never occurred to either of us to ask why certain kids from the same neighborhood went to some schools, and others could not.

It's just the way things were — until Marshall, until Mitchell.

What they gave my generation of children was the chance to work things out among ourselves, to break down the natural human suspicions of the unseen stranger. The system could reach us at an age when our way of looking at the world hadn't begun to calcify. We could see others for who they really were, and not what the whispers of adults tried to tell us they were.

As it happened, a new kind of public school segregation arrived not long after — one created not by laws but by the impossibility of changing so much history in a single generation.

Anxious white people conditioned to keep their distance from blacks found convenient real estate agents and took part in a massive exodus to surrounding suburban counties.

Today, at the turn of the century, the public schools of the city of Baltimore are nearly 90 percent black. But there is something else worth noting: In those suburban counties today, where a black middle-class migration followed the original white exodus, the population of the public schools generally reflects the racial percentages of the counties themselves.

Not only in metropolitan Baltimore — but in suburban communities around the country.

One generation learns a few things from the lessons, and the mistakes, of their elders.

Thurgood Marshall and Clarence Mitchell Jr. never said it would be easy.

They only insisted, against all odds and against all previous American history, that it was right.

Michael Olesker is a Sun *columnist and a graduate of the city's public schools. He is co-author (with Leo Bretholz) of "Leap Into Darkness," a Holocaust memoir, and author of "Michael Olesker's Baltimore: If You Live Here, You're Home."*

Health care architect

by M. William Salganik

HAL COHEN SAVED Marylanders $17.5 billion. To be sure, he had some help. But as the first executive director of the Health Services Cost Review Commission, he was a prime architect of a system which held down hospital costs in Maryland.

The commission's success also encouraged state lawmakers to enact other activist consumer legislation in health: "report cards" to measure care and member satisfaction with HMOs; an appeal process to challenge HMO decisions; a system to make insurance more affordable for small employers. Maryland's path to its present position as a state with aggressive health regulation – and proud of it – began with twin problems. Hospital costs here were among the highest in the nation, 25 percent above the national average. At the same time, urban hospitals, treating large numbers of uninsured patients, faced financial trouble. In 1971, the legislature voted to create the Health Services Cost Review Commission, with the seemingly contradictory goals of holding down costs while maintaining access for the uninsured and keeping hospitals solvent.

The commission decided to bring in a health economist. It turned to

PHOTO BY WALTER MCCARDELL, 1975

Harold Cohen

Harold A. Cohen, then teaching courses on government regulation at the University of Georgia. "I didn't know at all whether I would like being out of academe," he recalled. "I had always wanted to be a teacher."

He was so unsure that he didn't quit his teaching job – he took a two-year leave of absence.

The law he set out to implement was vague, deliberately so, specifying only the broad goals. "But that turned out to be one of the strong points of the law," Cohen noted in retrospect. "It's flexible. It tells you what you have to accomplish, but not how you have to accomplish it."

"Hal was the one who took a loosely worded piece of legislation and had a lot of flexibility to develop a payment system," said Larry Lawrence, a vice president of the Maryland Hospital Association.

Cohen began by attracting an intellectual staff, including two people with doctorates in advanced mathematics from Oxford University in England – not typical state bureaucrats. It wasn't the pay that lured them. "We used to joke about getting one-thousandth of one percent of what we saved, instead of the salaries we did get," Cohen says.

J. Graham Atkinson, one of those Oxford-trained mathematicians, said he was drawn by trying to solve a challenging problem, "largely by the fact that it was a wide-open field. And Hal was very different from the typical bureaucrat. He was willing and eager to attract new ideas."

Now a consultant to hospitals and health regulators, Atkinson remembers, "It was really exciting, because nobody had done anything like it before, and the regulatory tools were very primitive."

Cohen and his brain trust made the hospitals nervous. "There were a lot of mixed views" in the industry, Lawrence remembered. "Hal was a very bright young man who had a lot of radical ideas. He was very professorial. He didn't have any operational experience."

Aside from the clash of personalities, there were disagreements with the new commission over issues from insurers and hospitals. "The hospital industry looked on it as their right to be paid for their costs," Atkinson said. "The idea of somebody setting rates based on efficient production was quite shocking."

The commission charged ahead, holding hearings to set rates for each unit of service — a room day, a diagnostic test — at each of the state's 50 hospitals. Costs of treating the uninsured and of training residents and interns were built into the rates.

In the early years, it made two key changes in the system, adding an annual inflation adjustment to eliminate the need for time-consuming hearings for every hospital every year. And the commission encouraged efficiency by providing, in effect, rate bonuses for hospitals that controlled their average cost per case.

The results were dramatic. From 25 percent above the national average in 1976, the cost of an average hospital stay in Maryland dropped to 12 percent below the national average in 1992. If Maryland's costs had increased at the same rate as the rest of the country, the commission calculated, the state's residents would have paid $17.5 billion more for hospital care.

The uninsured continued to have access to all Maryland hospitals. Hospitals became stable financially. The commission gained acceptance. "By 1977 or 1978, there was terrific support for the commission," Lawrence said.

In effect, Cohen noted, the hospitals were offered solvency in exchange for efficiency. "I think it worked," he added, "because the hospitals bought into the idea that the trade-off was a good deal and that the targets were reasonable."

Cohen left the commission after 15 years, working as a consultant and serving on three federal commissions dealing with health. The commission's long run of success ended in the mid-1990s. Nationally, under pressure from HMOs, hospital costs did not increase at all, while Maryland's regulated rates continued to rise. The commission now has a task force studying "redesign" — and Cohen attends most of the meetings.

M. William Salganik covers the business of health and has been with The Sun *since 1977. He has also covered education and Baltimore city government. He was an editor of the Perspective section and an editor on the metropolitan desk.*

Educators of the century

by Mike Bowler

IN THE EARLY summer of 1999, I invited readers of my Education Beat column in *The Sun* to join me in choosing a "Maryland Educator of the Century."

My idea was simple and my rules few. I would make nominations regularly until the end of the year. Readers could second one of my suggestions by phone, letter or fax, or they could nominate independently. At the end of the year (and of the century), I would announce the consensus winner.

Nominees could be living or dead. The one and only rule was that they had to have lived at least half of their lives in the 20th century. This would disallow John F. Goucher, for example, but allow consideration of Edith Hamilton, the great classicist and 26-year headmistress of Bryn Mawr School.

My first two nominees were Philip H. "Doc" Edwards and Wilmer A. Dehuff, the revered mid-century principals of City College and Poly, respectively. What happened then was exactly what I had hoped. The City-Poly rivalry heated up, and I received dozens of "votes" from each camp, including 50 from a retirement community apparently populated by Poly alumni. I also got a touching letter from Edwards' 69-year-old granddaughter, living in Bermuda.

My thought upon launching the competition was that we would get into some serious discussion around the task of choosing a Marylander "of the century." Men and women are shaped by the times in which they live. Thomas G. Pullen Jr., state school superintendent for 22 years over mid-century, might have been the century's most influential holder of that job. Should his spotty record on school desegregation cost him some demerits?

As of late summer, there was little of that kind of discussion, perhaps because I didn't particularly encourage it. But what *did* happen was a pleasant surprise, even an inspiration.

A number of readers nominated one of their own teachers as Maryland Educator of the Century.

At first I was puzzled. I'd been thinking higher up the food chain: Edwards vs. Dehuff; Martin Jenkins, the great Morgan State president; Hans Froelicher, the man who brilliantly molded Park School; Benjamin Quarles, the renowned Morgan State historian. Mostly men.

Wilson Watson, a professor at the Catonsville campus of the Community College of Baltimore County, was thinking not smaller but differently. "As I look back on my 40 years of teaching English, first on the high school and then on the college level," he wrote, "I thank Frances Shores Meginnis for inspiring me to seek and demand excellence."

Meginnis had been Watson's English teacher at Towson High School more than 40 years ago. After I mentioned Watson's nomination, others like it followed. Readers described teachers who had molded and inspired them, given them the inspiration to enter a profession, in some cases to become teachers themselves.

And I began to think, "Why not?" Many — dare I say most? — of us have teachers of our lives, men and women who are part of our makeup, like parents and siblings. Perhaps these people, living and dead, are the Maryland Educators of the Century.

I'll nominate one as representative of the thousands of others.

When Mary Berry retired two years ago after 51 years in Harford County classrooms and public school libraries, 400 people, many of them former students, packed an Aberdeen ballroom to give her a send-off. (Among other farewell gifts was a trip to Paris, a vacation she's had to delay because of her husband's illness.)

"I was so happy to see them all," Berry said of her former students. "Some had said they couldn't come because they wanted to surprise me. But they came."

Berry, 74, attended "colored" schools in Harford and went to work at Central Consolidated in Bel Air, a strictly segregated school for blacks in grades one through 12. When she retired in 1997, Central was Hickory

Elementary, a modern elementary school with a new name, a good library and children the color of salt and pepper.

Berry has three children of her own: a preacher, an engineer and, of course, a teacher. Denise Berry is a team leader in mathematics at Sudbrook Academy in Baltimore County.

When I first interviewed Mary Berry a dozen years ago, she was worrying about her profession. "I hate to see so many good people turning away from teaching because the salaries are so low," she said. "You can't live in this society without money, but I think there are still more people than you think who genuinely want to help other people."

Little has changed, Berry said recently. "I still think teachers are underpaid for the long hours they have to put in."

But in the end, well worth it. "There's no greater feeling than standing on the stage at graduation time and realizing that you contributed to their hopes and dreams. It's the only thing I ever wanted to do."

Mike Bowler has been a reporter, editorial writer, opinion-page editor and education editor for the Evening Sun *and* The Sun *since 1970.*

A judicial craftsman's steady hand

by J. S. Bainbridge Jr.

WHEN HE WAS Maryland's chief judge, few would recognize Robert C. Murphy Jr. on one of his midday walks near the Towson courthouse. But anyone who had gone to Traffic Court in the last couple of decades, filed a lawsuit as a victim of intentional emotional abuse, or attended an Orioles game at Camden Yards had been touched by him.

By the time he reached 70 — the mandatory retirement age for Maryland judges — in 1996, Murphy had overseen Maryland's court system for a quarter-century, not as a caretaker but as a master craftsman.

He transformed the way justice works in this state. His replacement as chief judge called Murphy "the father of the modern Maryland judiciary."

He even affected the color of every state law library collection. Until computers take over completely, green rows of volumes containing published decisions of the Court of Special Appeals — Maryland's intermediate appellate court — will line bookshelves. Murphy was the first chief judge of that court, and his Irish heritage inspired him to choose emerald green as the proper color to bind those opinions.

Murphy was no patrician. The son of a B&O Railroad detective's son, he used to sneak into the racetrack in his Pimlico neighborhood, just avoiding getting nabbed by police a few times.

He earned both his college and law school degrees locally before being chosen as a law clerk in the U.S. Court of Customs and Patent Appeals in Washington, now the U.S. Court of Appeals for the Federal Circuit.

Soon he began working in the Maryland attorney general's office, eventually rising to deputy attorney general where he ran the office. He served temporarily for three months as attorney general before his appointment as chief judge of the Court of Special Appeals in 1967. Five years later, Murphy was named Court of Appeals chief judge; at 45, he was the youngest person in state history to hold the job.

From the moment he took office, Murphy transformed the state's judicial system. A District Court had just been set up to replace the fractured, often corrupt collection of lower-level courts. This new statewide system was led by tough, savvy Robert F. Sweeney, a colleague of Murphy's from their days together running the attorney general's office.

Together the two jovial and politically savvy Irishmen made the new system work, with every District Court judge from the Eastern Shore to the mountains west of Cumberland adhering to impartial standards with directives from Annaapolis.

Murphy's predecessor as chief judge had been Hall Hammond, a stern, austere scholar whose opinions were respected. He had little interest, though, in overseeing Maryland's judiciary. Murphy, in contrast, had a passion and talent for administration that became crucial as shock waves from the litigation explosion of recent decades were felt.

PHOTO BY RICHARD CHILDRESS, 1981

Hon. Robert C. Murphy Jr.

In 1970, the state court system had 89 judges and a budget of $4 million. Murphy built support staff and lobbied hard for new judgeships. When he retired, 260 judges sat on the Maryland bench and the judiciary's budget was $169 million.

Under Murphy's leadership, courts started using computers,

the judicial pension system was improved, and retired judges were brought back to help ease the caseloads of active jurists.

Where Hammond stayed away from the legislative branch, Murphy walked the halls each General Assembly session, charming lawmakers with his easy manner, coaxing them to allocate cash to the courts. His integrity and approachability were unquestioned.

Yet Murphy still managed his full load as a Court of Appeals judge. He wrote over 1,000 opinions in cases ranging from the constitutional requirements of public school funding to the legal justification for authorizing construction of Oriole Park at Camden Yards to recognizing intentional infliction of emotional distress as a cause of action.

Unlike other judges, Murphy could never be typed as liberal or conservative. He was a consensus-builder, who would avoid entrenched positions for the sake of reaching what he saw as a fair, acceptable result.

Murphy's affability was no act. He reveled in the variety of people he came in contact with, taking a personal interest in everyone, including those who could offer him nothing in return.

In retirement, while working on decisions that had been argued when he was a sitting judge, Murphy started telling a clerk about the teenage daughter of a lower-level courthouse employee. She played sports in high school, but a problem with her spine put her in the hospital over the Christmas holidays.

"Julie," he called to his secretary, "Let's give her something. A basket of fruit."

"Judge," she answered, "the court has already sent her a basket."

"Well, that was the court," Murphy said. "I'm retired. I want to send something from me."

J. S. Bainbridge Jr., a lawyer, was a Sun *reporter from 1973 to 1984. He covered legal affairs.*

Protecting our natural heritage

by Tom Horton

FEW READERS WILL know Joe and Ilia Fehrer, citizens of Snow Hill. But many will know and love the great cypress swamps and dark waters of the Pocomoke River, which would be much diminished but for the Fehrers' often thankless and voluntary environmentalism for three decades.

Across Maryland, one could make so many similar statements about environmentalists — my Marylanders of the Century — our collective conscience in protecting the state's natural heritage.

There is Judy Johnson and Assateague Island National Seashore; Dan Boone and Beth Hartline and Western Maryland's wildest forestlands.

Jim Gracie and Richard Klein, whose leadership in the unsexy areas of sediment and storm water control translates to clearer, cleaner water in thousands of miles of streams; Lina Vlavianos, advocate for little Jabez Branch, a lovely trout stream surviving against all odds, hard by I-97 in Anne Arundel County.

Dan Boone, a naturalist who has roamed every corner of the state, identifying areas of special value. Again and again, when you research the history of how natural treasures got protected, you find Boone was there first.

Also, Bonnie Bick and Alex Winter, who raised such a ruckus the state had no choice but to preserve miles of mature, forested Potomac River shorelines nearly within sight of Washington, D.C.

And Nick Carter, a state biologist who, for a generation or more, has tackled the tough issues, from population control and overdevelopment to agricultural drainage ditching.

There are better known members among the state's assembly of environmental heroes: former Gov. Harry R. Hughes, whose administration shaped the legislation that guides Chesapeake Bay restoration 17 years later (for all that, what impresses me most about Hughes is that he continues, in retirement, working hard on environmental issues back home on the Eastern Shore).

Two farmers — the late state treasurer and Senate president, William S. James, and retired state Senate president James Clark Jr. — arguably did more than most to preserve the landscape by passing Program Open Space, a dedicated fund that, 30 years later, has acquired 10 percent of the state.

Russell Train, the first Environmental Protection Agency administrator, and the Eastern Shore's late Rep. Rogers C. B. Morton, whose initials didn't stand for Chesapeake Bay (but could have) are other Maryland environmentalists of note. Chandler Robbins, a biologist at Patuxent Wildlife Research Center, is a world renowned ornithologist, and just as devoted to the birds of Maryland.

There is also Patrick Noonan, founder of The Nature Conservancy and, more recently The Conservation Fund, which engineered the biggest land buy in Maryland history, putting nearly 100 square miles in public ownership forever.

One could make a "Marylander" case for Rachel Carson, who lived and worked and attended graduate school in the state for a time. Her book, "Silent Spring" published in 1962, was one of the most influential environmental works of the century.

But more than the luminaries it is the little people, working in relative obscurity, often spending half a lifetime just to improve and protect their own backyards and neighborhoods, that seem to me the strength of modern environmentalism.

"Think globally, act locally" is a slogan that emerged from the movement. It is hard to improve on that.

Coalescing around the time of the first Earth Day in 1970, environmentalism marked a fundamental departure from old-style "conservation" (as in farmers conserving topsoil and duck hunters conserving wetlands), worthy as those aims may be.

Environmentalism saw nature ecologically, intimately inter-connected, connected to all human actions, and critically in need of protection almost everywhere — protection that often disconcerted those pursuing business as usual.

Eventually, the environmental movement may be seen as the beginning of extending rights to nature, just as most civilized societies have extended rights to women and minorities.

So the century list of Marylander-environmentalists-heroes continues:

In environmental education, with the late Arthur Sherwood, who founded the hugely successful Chesapeake Bay Foundation. Also the late Gene Cronin, leading bay scientist for decades, who tirelessly educated Congress, the media, environmentalists and all others who would listen to the workings of his native Chesapeake.

Sustaining the environmental movement through its formative years were people like the late Frances Froelicher, founder of the old Better Air Coalition in Baltimore, and William Goodman, Armin Behr and Ajax Eastman, with the Maryland Conservation Council.

A consistent and tireless force for the last two decades in networking environmental, business and agricultural interests has been Frances Flanigan, head of the Alliance for the Chesapeake Bay.

Two other parties must be included in this century-fest:

A sizable number of hard-working bureaucrats in Maryland's Department of Natural Resources and Department of the Environment. There is more dedication, talent and late-night hours put in there than the public ever realizes, or the media credits.

Finally, Tom Wisner, the Chesapeake singer, storyteller and poet, whose heartfelt performances over the decades have inspired a considerable number of all those listed above.

Tom Horton began covering the environment for The Sun *in 1975. He writes the "Around the Bay" column for* The Sun *and is the author of five books about the Chesapeake Bay.*

A principled senator

by Peter J. Kumpa

MILLARD E. TYDINGS, Maryland's champion of Jeffersonian Democratic principles, never ran from a fight. One of the U.S. Senate's "Big Mules," he was the independent-minded political leader who more than stood his ground in two sensational and nasty fights against Franklin D. Roosevelt at the height of the New Deal and against Sen. Joseph McCarthy in the early days of the Cold War.

A conservative but loyal Democrat, Tydings had backed much of Roosevelt's New Deal policies, though he opposed excessive deficit spending. But in 1937, he rallied opposition to Roosevelt's plan to add four more justices to the Supreme Court. It was too much power for one man. Throughout his career, Tydings was suspicious of too much power in the hands of dictators abroad or presidents at home.

A year later, Roosevelt worked to "purge" Tydings from the Senate, backing Democratic Rep. David J. Lewis, a liberal from Western Maryland. FDR campaigned personally in Maryland. But Tydings not only won easily but received a handful of votes in the 1940 Democratic National Convention opposing Roosevelt's third-term presidency.

When McCarthy alleged that the State Department was crawling with card-carrying Communists, Tydings was designated to look into the accusations. He found not "an ounce of truth" in the charges which he described as "a fraud, a hoax and a deceit."

McCarthy then went after Tydings in the infamous 1950 campaign when Tydings was seeking a fifth term. Literature was distributed with composite photos purporting to show Tydings in intimate conversation with Earl Browder, the U.S. leader of the Communist Party. Maryland voters, in this critical battle, let Tydings down. He lost what historians consider one of the dirtiest campaigns in American history.

When he was in the U.S. House of Representatives in 1924, Tydings defended the position of his state's leaders in opposing Prohibition. He felt Prohibition had not accomplished its goals. He preferred state's rights to such sweeping national policy.

Tydings had a sweep of accomplishments that would put him in any political Hall of Fame, national or state. His most important legislation was the establishment of an effective Department of Defense, bringing all the military services together under single leadership.

One of the genuine heroes of the ugly trench warfare of World War I, Tydings fought isolationists to improve American preparedness before the next world conflict. He was the leading voice for a big navy. He supported fortifying Guam, expanding the Panama Canal and strengthening the army. When asked why he backed Selective Service, Tydings replied, "I would rather have it and not need it, than need it and not have it."

During World War II, Tydings worked to eliminate waste and inefficiency from the ballooning wartime bureaucracy. After the war, he supported policies to aid Greece and Turkey and to fund the Marshall Plan to move Europe from desolation to economic recovery. He had investigated the grim conditions in ten countries. His testimony was influential in Senate approval of generous foreign aid. He argued it was cheaper than another war.

More than any other figure, Tydings was responsible for the independence of The Philippines and spoke at independence ceremonies there in 1946.

For all his expertise in national and international affairs, Tydings' most lasting contribution was his consistent and articulate exposition of the conservative Democratic philosophy. Overwhelmed in New Deal days by Democratic liberals, the Tydings view of balanced budgets, small government, protection of business, balanced government between all of its branches — these are the fundamentals that would be centrist or moderate today. The politics of inclusion would have appealed to Tydings. It meant to him that conservatives were as welcome in the Democratic Party as any other point of view, and it was a party that he never considered leaving.

Tydings traced his Harford County ancestors to John O'Neill, who had battled against the British attack on Havre de Grace in 1813. He served in Maryland's Blue and Gray 29th Division in World War I, enlisting as a private and mustering out as a much-decorated lieutenant colonel. War in the trenches transformed him into a man in cool command.

Before the war, he had been elected to the House of Delegates. When he returned as a war hero, he became speaker of the House in 1920. He sponsored the bill creat-

PHOTO BY RALPH DOHME, 1956

Millard and Eleanor Tydings

ing the University of Maryland. He moved on to the state Senate, then to the U.S. House for two terms before winning four terms in the U.S. Senate.

It was Tydings who sponsored legislation making the Star Spangled Banner the National Anthem.

Tydings was prescient about how the world was turning. He predicted in 1927 that "communism will not survive" and that it would evolve eventually into capitalism. He denounced Hitler's takeover of Germany as a "crime against civilizations" and denounced Nazi persecution of Catholics and Jews.

It was his analytical ability on a broad range of issues that won him respect from his colleagues. But the tall, square-jawed Tydings, who liked to sport white-linen suits in summer, was also feared for a slashing oratorical style tinged with arrogance.

Millard Tydings died in 1961, a man of independence and principle. He was Maryland's most powerful national legislator in the century. His widow, Eleanor Davies Tydings, said that his three loves were his country, his state and the U.S. Senate. "I am proud," she said, "to have been his fourth love."

Peter J. Kumpa's career at The Sun *spanned over 40 years as a* Sun *foreign correspondent, Washington Bureau chief and local political columnist for the* Evening Sun.

It's for you, sport

by James H. Bready

SOMETIME SOON, THE Marketing Department will decide that Maryland needs a new slogan. Old Line State, Free State, Land of Pleasant Living? Not much sells there, by third-millennium standards. We need something catchier.

What, then, distinguishes modern Maryland? Physical games.

We play everything, from marbles in childhood to retirement's duffer golf. Both genders. Competitively, recreationally. And, just as important, we pause to watch the people who play so well as to make their living from it.

Maryland: It's For You, Sport.

We didn't used to be so athletic; it just happened, during the 1900s. It happened in every other state, too; but, small though we are, Maryland simply has the varied land and water, the change of seasons, the close-byness for pretty near any game you can think of. Not a whole lot of fishing in Kansas; in Maine, bocce's not big, nor is spelunking.

California's southern end has more everyday balm, true; but by now, climate control counts for more — everywhere, a large part of sport goes on indoors, and right on schedule, so long as the electricity's working.

(It is an odd boast — games galore — for a state without a domed stadium.)

Often, sports comparisons take the low, numbers road: how many Big Four (baseball, football, basketball, ice hockey) franchises have you? How many championship teams, Olympic gold medalists, world-record holders?

A better way to look at it would be to compare percentages of the day spent playing, or training, or watching. (Does it count, calling in on sports radio, or holding the bets in sports bars?) But this, the ever-inquisitive poll-takers seem not yet to have gotten around to.

Any such mathematics, then, has to allow for population disparities. Does Maryland have more baseball Hall of Fame members per 1,000 residents than 49 other states do? The road to nowhere: who has title to Babe Ruth, for instance, Maryland or New York?

The real point is to encourage young Marylanders, and people arrived from elsewhere, to flex here (and, sport being sport, to sharpen their strategies here). And, while we spectators are at it, to send up a few more cheers. A good way to do this is to think back across a hundred calendars, to glow at thought of this hero, of that team or coach, of the upset triumph that is ours, all ours.

Joe Gans. John Unitas. Slade Cutter. Jim Lacy. Eddie Hurt. Spike Webb. Curley Byrd. Joe Bellino. Toots Barger. Lefty Reitz. Native Dancer. Doug and Jack Turnbull. Bob Scott. Gardner Mallonee. Lefty Grove. Charles Garland. Cal Ripken Jr. Jack Dunn's Seven Straighters. Dick Harlow's Green Terrors. Harold Baines. All baseball's best ballpark (twice). Jim Tatum's Sugar Bowlers.

The blank space is for you to write down your favorites.

Consider that ultimate footrace, the marathon, which ends with one winner, 999 losers. But those same two or three hours can produce any number of personal-best clockings. In sport, tomorrow matters more than yesterday. Even if you, a lifelong Marylander, lack all athletic urge, no harm done. If you do have the sports gene but weren't yet corporeal, during Sudden Death in 1958, or the fourth game of the 1966 World Series, you can make up for it; just listen. Just read, watch, play.

Cross country. Cycling. Soccer, softball, swimming, skiing, sailing, sky-diving, skeet-shooting. Lacrosse. Tennis. Field hockey. Hang-gliding. From archery to yachting, we got 'em all. (Luge? Uh, no.) Duckpins. Handball. Badminton. Jousting, jumping, animal-judging. Fencing, wrestling (amateurs only), squash. Horsehoe-pitching. Volleyball. Weightlifting. Rowing, diving, surfing, water-skiing, figure-skating. Rock-climbing. Table tennis and timber racing. Gymnastics and canoeing.

The blank space, again, is for your use, hailing your game. Maryland. Get ready. Get set. Go!

James H. Bready, a retired Evening Sun *editorial writer and columnist, continues to write a column on local books, which he began in 1954. His latest book is "Baseball in Baltimore: The First 100 Years."*

Overlooked pioneer of cardiac surgery

by Glenn McNatt

AT A TIME when most African-American men were doing well if they could find employment as Pullman-car porters or postal employees, Vivien Thomas was quietly laying the foundations for modern cardiac surgery.

With neither a medical diploma nor even a college degree, Thomas devised a now widely used surgical technique to treat "blue baby" syndrome, a congenital heart defect that prevents blood from reaching the lungs.

Although credit for this medical breakthrough has often been given exclusively to the noted pediatrician Dr. Helen Taussig and Dr. Alfred Blalock, both of Johns Hopkins Hospital, Thomas played a decisive role in developing the procedure — a role that until recently has been all but ignored.

In 1944, Taussig asked Blalock, who was already renowned for his research in shock trauma, what could be done to prolong the lives of children born with blue-baby syndrome.

Thomas, who was Blalock's invaluable research assistant, immediately undertook a series of experiments on lab animals to determine if it was possible to reroute the plumbing of a human heart.

Thomas had worked with Blalock for more than a decade when he set to

PHOTO BY RICHARD CHILDRESS, 1976

Vivien Thomas

solve this problem. Born in New Iberia, La., Thomas had once dreamed of being a physician himself, but the Depression forced him to find work as a carpenter. In 1930, Thomas learned of an opening in the medical laboratory at Vanderbilt University and applied for the job.

Blalock, who headed the lab, apparently sensed the potential of the young Thomas and hired him as his assistant. Thomas quickly mastered every aspect of the lab's routine, excelling in anatomy and physiology and making himself indispensable to Blalock's research program.

The two made an unlikely pair. Blalock was the proud scion of a prominent old Southern family. Thomas was a modest, unassuming man with a wife and children to support. But they worked well together, and the shock trauma research they conducted at Vanderbilt eventually helped save the lives of thousands of American soldiers during World War II.

When Blalock received an offer to come to Hopkins in 1941, Thomas accompanied him to Baltimore.

To devise a procedure for treating heart defects in humans, Thomas experimented on hundreds of lab animals and perfected the intricate techniques required on dogs first at the old Hunterian lab on the Johns Hopkins medical campus. After satisfying himself that every contingency was accounted for, he taught the entire exacting procedure to Blalock, who would perform the actual surgery.

Early on the morning of Nov. 29, 1944, Blalock and his surgical team gathered in the operating room to perform the first cardiac surgery on a child, 15-month-old Eileen Saxon. When the operation began, Thomas took his customary place in the balcony above the operating room floor to watch the procedure he had created unfold.

But before Blalock even made the first incision, he called Thomas to his side. Thomas came down from the balcony and stood on a small footstool behind Blalock's right shoulder, a position that allowed him to see clearly every detail of the operation's progress.

Throughout the surgery, Blalock frequently consulted Thomas as he worked through the intricate procedure. The operation lasted three hours and was deemed a complete success. Over the next several days, little baby Eileen's complexion gradually turned from pale blue to a healthy pink. Thomas later said the transformation was "almost a miracle."

The success of the operation gave new hope to parents of blue babies, and the hospital was soon inundated with requests for the live-saving operation. Thomas and Blalock had opened up a new medical specialty, modern cardiac surgery.

For 30 years before Johns Hopkins admitted its first black surgical resident in 1971, Thomas taught the procedures he had developed to the hospital's white surgeons. Among Thomas' many contributions to medicine was his invention of a respirator that allowed his animal patients to breathe during experimental surgery by inflating their lungs. This technology was later successfully applied to human patients.

Thomas continued as Blalock's assistant until Blalock's retirement in 1964, after which he remained at Hopkins to supervise the surgical laboratories for another 15 years. In 1976, one of his lifelong dreams was finally realized when the university awarded him an honorary doctorate, and in 1977 he was appointed to the medical school faculty.

Thomas died in 1985, still largely unknown outside the small circle of "old hands" at Hopkins who had witnessed his genius.

Vivien Thomas was a great man motivated by the possibilities of discovery, but he lived in an age when black men, no matter how gifted, were largely invisible. It has taken more than half a century for the true dimensions of his contributions finally to be appreciated and for Thomas to take his place among the giants of 20th-century medicine.

Glenn McNatt is The Sun's *art critic and previously wrote editorials at the newspaper.*

More deserving Marylanders

by Barry Rascovar

NOW I KNOW what judges in the Miss America pageant go through. It's agonizing selecting from all the beauties parading before you.

Only 21 people made it onto the editorial pages as *The Sun's* "Marylanders of the Century." Yet so many more deserved the recognition that I had no trouble compiling a second list of significant achievers.

Even then, worthy men and women had to be omitted, such as former Sen. Charles McC. Mathias; writer and headmistress Edith Hamilton; Cardinal Lawrence Shehan; Commercial Credit founder Alexander Duncan; writers Anne Tyler and John Barth; and Orioles Hall of Famer Brooks Robinson.

Here's how I would make the original list of 21 into a compendium of 42:

Politicians Millard E. Tydings, William S. James and Helen Delich Bentley (she qualifies in the journalist category, too).

Civil rights lobbyist Clarence M. Mitchell Jr.

Business visionaries Frank Perdue, Glenn L. Martin, Alonzo G. Decker, T. Rowe Price and J. Willard Marriott Sr.

Arts and letters contributors Etta Cone, Rosa Ponselle, Lizette Woodworth Reese and Joseph Meyerhoff (also on the best-in-business list).

Environmental-muckraker Rachel Carson.

Medical pioneers R. Adams Cowley and William H. Welch.

Journalists A. Aubrey Bodine and Carl J. Murphy.

Educators Harry C. Byrd and Mary L. Titcomb.

Sports legend John Unitas.

In brief, here's why each of these Marylanders deserves inclusion:

• **Millard Tydings.** A conservative Democrat from Havre de Grace, he served four terms in the U.S. Senate, took on Sen. Joseph McCarthy and his wild accusations of communist infiltration of government; stood up to President Franklin D. Roosevelt; crusaded for Philippine independence and for U.S. aid to rebuild Europe after World War II.

• **William James.** A genteel, scholarly man, he was a dominant force in Annapolis for over four decades, especially as Senate president. He spearheaded the drive for a statewide community college system and for Program Open Space, which has preserved 189,000 acres of land from development. It's a national model.

• **Helen Bentley.** A pioneering journalist for *The Sun*, she became the best-known maritime writer in the nation. For half a century she's been a ceaseless, dogged advocate for the Port of Baltimore in print, on television, as chairman of the Federal Maritime Commission and as a five-term member of Congress.

• **Clarence Mitchell Jr.** The most influential lobbyist in Washington during the great civil-rights advances of the 1960s. His children and grandchildren have built a formidable political dynasty in West Baltimore.

• **Frank Perdue.** In three decades, he turned a small Salisbury egg business into one of the country's biggest chicken operations. Through creative advertising ("It takes a tough man to raise a tender chicken"), Perdue convinced meat-eating Americans to switch to poultry.

• **Glenn L. Martin.** Seventy years after he built an aircraft plant in Middle River, it still thrives. Martin was a true aviation pioneer whose massive hangers once employed 53,000 people during World War II. His original company now is called Lockheed Martin, the country's largest aerospace firm.

• **Alonzo Decker.** He changed the way people work, by manufacturing handy construction equipment. Then he inaugurated an era of do-it-yourself home repairs with Black & Decker's easy to use tools.

• **T. Rowe Price.** Mutual funds and growth-stock investing bear his imprimatur. Wall Street's "Sage of Baltimore" started his company during the Depression. It is now one of the nation's largest and most respected mutual-fund investment firms.

• **J. Willard Marriott Sr.** From a nine-seat root-beer stand and a Hot Shoppe restaurant in 1927, he fashioned a food and lodging giant. Today's Marriott International offers travelers a choice of 1,500 hotels worldwide, with headquarters in Bethesda.

• **Etta Cone.** She and her sister, Claribel, gave to the Baltimore Museum of Art one of the most important and largest collections of Impressionist art. It made the BMA's reputation. The Cone apartment, overlooking Druid Hill Park, became a mini-museum and salon for the artistic world in the 1920s, 1930s and 1940s.

• **Rosa Ponselle.** Perhaps the greatest American operatic voice of this century, she ruled the Metropolitan Opera for nearly two decades, then became the guiding light of the Baltimore Opera Company.

• **Lizette Woodworth Reese.** This Western High School teacher wrote some of this country's finest lyrical poetry. In the first half of this century, American school children memorized her "Tears" poem. Her intensely felt sonnets reveal beauty even in common things.

• **Joseph Meyerhoff.** He'll be remembered for the money he spent to make the Baltimore Symphony Orchestra first-rate, then giving it a sparkling concert hall. But he also was one of the great home builders in the post-World War II era (along with Keelty and Knott), accounting for 15,000 single-family residences in the Baltimore area.

• **Rachel Carson.** Few books have started a revolution. Carson's "Silent Spring" sounded the alarm of environmental dangers in 1962. It's been the Bible for ecological reforms on a worldwide scale.

• **Dr. R Adams Cowley.** His unconventional ideas transformed shock-trauma medicine. Cowley had to take on the medical and political establishments in his fight to turn University of Maryland Hospital into the cutting-edge leader in comprehensive trauma care.

• **Dr. William C. Welch.** He organized the new Johns Hopkins Hospital, established the nation's first school of public health and hired the physicians who would revolutionize medicine, particularly Dr. William Osler and Dr. William S. Halsted.

• **A. Aubrey Bodine.** He gave us 50 years of photographic masterpieces that captured the human and physical beauty of Maryland for future generations to savor. This *Sun* photographer turned picture-taking for a daily newspaper into an art form.

• **Carl J. Murphy.** The *Afro-American* became one of the nation's most influential black newspapers under his guidance. He was a potent behind-the-scenes force in the local civil-rights movement.

• **Harry "Curley" Byrd.** Sure, he coached the University of Maryland football team to greatness, but his lasting contribution came as college president at College Park. He engineered a five-fold increase in students (to 16,000), a seven-fold budget increase and an 11-fold increase in the value of the college's physical plant. He used his clout in Annapolis to turn a "cow college" into a major university.

• **Mary L. Titcomb.** This innovative Hagerstown librarian started the first bookmobile in 1904, which for most of this century brought the world of literature to the nation's rural countryside and growing suburbs.

• **John Unitas.** He revolutionized professional football, propelling it into the television era with the championship Baltimore Colts. Simply the greatest quarterback to play the game. His daring on the field changed the nature of pro football.

There you have it: 21 Free State men and women to join the 21 others chosen by *The Sun's* editorial board as the best of the last 100 years. The question now becomes: Who will make the next list to be drawn up — of the top Marylanders of the 21st Century?

Index
of
Names

About the Editor

Barry Rascovar, deputy editorial page editor of *The Baltimore Sun*, is the author of "The Great Game of Maryland Politics." His weekly Sunday column has been a staple of Maryland politics for over two decades. A native Baltimorean, Mr. Rascovar graduated from Forest Park High School in the city. He majored in history at Dickinson College in Carlisle, Pa., then earned a master's degree, with honors, from the Columbia University Graduate School of Journalism in New York.

He's been a reporter and editor for *The Baltimore Sun* since 1969, covering politics and government at City Hall, at the Annapolis State House and in Washington.

Mr. Rascovar and his wife, the former Cecelia Hudson, reside in Baltimore County.